The Cruel Mother

The Cruel Mother

A family ghost laid to rest

Siân Busby

✳ SHORT BOOKS

First published in 2004 by
Short Books
15 Highbury Terrace
London N5 1UP

10 9 8 7 6 5 4 3 2 1

A CIP catalogue record for this book
is available from the British Library.

ISBN 1-904095-71-2

Printed in Great Britain by
Mackays, Chatham, Kent

In loving memory of R J W Wood (1902-1978)

She lean'd her back unto a thorn;
   Fine flowers in the valley
And there she has her two babes born,
   And the leaves they grow rarely.

She's ta'en the ribbon from her hair,
   Fine flowers in the valley
And bound their bodies fast and sure.
   And the leaves they grow rarely.

She's buried them both beneath the briar,
   Fine flowers in the valley
And washed her hands with many a tear.
   And the leaves they grow rarely.

The Cruel Mother, traditional ballad

PROLOGUE

I was a teenager when my mother's father died back in the late 1970s, and my cousins and I helped to tidy out his home. At one end of the dingy hallway, in a damp alcove, my grandfather had stacked up a pile of objects salvaged it seemed from the unravelling edge of his life. Together my cousins and I dutifully picked through what was for the most part worthless, dust-encrusted junk. We were looking out for anything of value, anything which would give us an insight into the man, give us back a piece of his long-lost life. Of course, characteristically, my grandfather receded from us with each new discovery. There was a 16mm film projector, the colour of a battleship with orange spots of rust congressing on its surface, some damp cartons of pianola rolls, hand-tinted photographic plates of floral arrangements and his old back garden in Camden Town, a World War Two gas mask, photographs of attractive women, and a battered leather briefcase full of insignia from the Ancient Order of the Water Buffalos. But nowhere was there a trace of anything relating to the single event which had exerted the greatest force over his life. We placed anything interesting to one side, and put everything else in a series of large black bin-bags.

At the very bottom of the pile we came upon a series of large, shallow cardboard boxes. They were tied with the same creamy silk ribbon which my grandfather had once tied around his fancy hatboxes during the few years, back in the 1940s, when he had been a successful West End milliner. We ripped open the boxes one after another, pulling off the ribbons without bothering to undo the bows, carelessly discarding the lids. Inside, nestling in snow-white tissue paper, were pieces of delicate netting, hat veils, scattered with coloured sequins. Each time we opened a box we watched for a few moments as the netting, finally exposed to the air for the first time in thirty years, dissolved into fragments before our eyes.

At times the process of writing this book has been a lot like gathering the broken shards of an old mirror in the hope of reassembling a reflection of the past. Much of what follows has had to be, to some extent, confabulation; for however certain I am of the facts, however verifiable my certainties have proved to be, the life of a dead ordinary person – even if like my great-grandmother, Beth, they did something extraordinary – is a very difficult thing to delineate. In truth, all I know for certain is how it turned out. For us – we who live in the present – the past is a foregone conclusion, and as we sift through the fragments left for us

in the bottom of boxes we are already shaping the outcome.

I have from time to time caught a glimpse of the ghosts
flitting between the lines, shivered as they whispered in my
ears in record offices and libraries, marvelled as they
seemed to place long-lost pieces of the puzzle in my hand.
But mostly I have had nothing to go on but the shrink-
wrapped memories of others, second, third, fourth-hand-
hand-me-downs – and my own sense of shared experience,
of common ground and blood. Maybe we are primed to
recognise the similarities between past lives and our own,
to filter out the strange and home in on the recognisable.
Perhaps the only reason we bother with the past at all is
because we are egotistically looking for clues about ourselves, seeking out our own hidden meaning and secret
purpose. If so, I have been as eager as anyone to grasp the
lifelines one generation throws across to another.

When I settled down to finally uncover the truth of the
single event in my great-grandmother's life which cast such
a shadow over her, her children and grandchildren and even
her great-grandchildren, I did not entertain a single doubt
about my right to do so; as I progressed there were many
times when I wondered whether I was doing the right thing.
The generations between Beth's and my own had taken so
much trouble to tidy everything away that I sometimes felt
like a spoilt kid, rummaging, wrecking, exposing fragile
items to the air only to watch them crumble away. At the
end of the process, while I am sorry if there are any mem-

bers of my family who feel that perhaps, after all, this dirty corner of our common past was best left unaired, I have come to believe that it is better to lift the edge of the carpet, to let the dust fly.

And what about Beth? Where is she in all of this? Well, I started out simply wanting to find out why she did what she did: to try and understand. But I realise now that this book has been my way of letting her know that she is, finally, forgiven. After all, it is because of everything that happened that we are as we are, and still the future beckons.

SEB
London, 2004

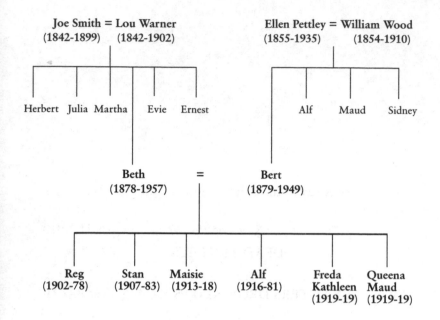

Joe Smith = Lou Warner
(1842-1899)   (1842-1902)

Herbert Julia Martha Evie Ernest

Ellen Pettley = William Wood
(1855-1935)   (1854-1910)

Alf Maud Sidney

Beth   =   Bert
(1878-1957)   (1879-1949)

Reg   Stan   Maisie   Alf   Freda   Queena
(1902-78)   (1907-83)   (1913-18)   (1916-81)   Kathleen   Maud
                                                  (1919-19)   (1919-19)

-1-

"Bert says I have drowned the babies...."

News of the World, August 31, 1919

DEAD TRIPLETS

TWO BABY SISTERS DROWNED IN BACKYARD BATH

Triplet girls born to Mr. and Mrs. B. W. Wood, of London-road, Romford, a little over a week ago, are all dead, two of them under tragic circumstances. The first died shortly after birth, but the others and the mother seemed to be going on fairly well. Early one morning Mrs. Wood called her husband and saying she had been bathing the children, asked for them. The father could not see them in the house. Going into the yard he found them, both dead, in a bath of rain water.

The first thought I had when I found the article on the microfilm was that Grandma Wood had drowned only two of her babies, and not all three as we had always been told.

And that they were girls, not boys. My grandfather's twin sisters.... my mother's aunts....

Then it dawned on me that after all this time there it was in black and white right in front of me. Now I knew for sure. It was no family myth, no story embellished and garbled through the passage of time, no terrible lie, no daydream or nightmare. It had really happened.

***

Romford, Autumn 1939

Dear Reg,

Just a few lines hoping they will find you well. We have been waiting to hear what you are doing. Hope you are getting along alright.

Have you heard from Ettie and the children. Hope they are all well and liking Wales.

Things seem in a terrible muddle don't they.

How did you get on over the road last Wednesday week. Dad was just getting up when the sirens went.

I felt rotten for two or three days after but after the all clear went I went down to the Drill Hall and saw the troops go from here & I think I caught the sun. It was very Hot.

My head and neck have ached ever since. This war business gets one down doesn't it.

Dad told me dinner time Uncle Sid went in the yard this morning. 40 have got the sack in his firm & he is

*among the unlucky ones. He said he don't know what
they will do.*

*I guess there is a good many don't know what they will
do...*

*So sorry the weather seems to have left us. But we may
have another spell again.*

Let us have a line letting us know what you are doing.

*Must close for the present. What do you think of the
blackout at night. Hope you are not out in it.*

Much love until I see you

Mum

    xxx

      ***

That first summer after the Great War, in 1919, when it
really did seem as if the world was coming to an end, it was
like moving through a dream. They kept on about the
future, and building a land fit for heroes, yet looking
around it was hard to have any faith in what we were all
coming to. Things were in a terrible mess. It wasn't even as
if the war was over – not really – when there were still
heaps of men away: in hospitals at the Front, in Russia, in
prison camps. And those who had made it back were in no
shape to start rebuilding the nation.

You saw them everywhere, gibbering wrecks for the
most part, bandaged stumps where hands and feet had
once been, eyes milky white and sightless. Horrible to see

it. And most of them no more than kids. Mind you, those who had come through it in one piece were not much better: angry and kicking up a terrible fuss, shouting about this and that, skulking about with nothing better to do than thieve and drink, or stand about half-starved on street corners trying to sell the boots off their feet. That summer after the war there was ruin everywhere you looked. It was enough to get you down; it really was.

And yet, awful as things were, you had to keep up appearances: it still mattered what other people thought of you. Most of the time what other people thought about you was the only thing that kept you whole. It made you get up in the mornings, and you did that even though what you really wanted was to chuck it all in, put an end to the worry, the uncertainty; an end to wondering whether you and yours would get by and things would ever be the same again, like they were before. You looked about you and you couldn't help but think, there's a good many here that's staring ruin in the face and how can you be sure that you are not one of them?

Beth couldn't begin to tell how many times she wished she were dead and out of it all – like that was the only way to get rid of the awful feeling that something dreadful was going to happen. No fighting it, the feelings just came upon her against her will. But she knew that you had to keep on going. She was no worse off than anyone else. You just had to get on with it. It was what was expected.

By four o'clock that morning the sunlight was already

beginning to seep into all the secret corners of the back-yard, finding out the mossy cracks in between the bricks, and the air was thick enough to muffle every sound that cleaved to it. The old mule must have snorted as the latch on the shed door was lifted, but she didn't remember hearing him, not then anyway; as far as she could tell nothing else living was awake.

The bath hung on an old nail behind the door. How did she find the strength to lift it down and drag it all the way across the yard? It was a full-sized galvanised tin bath and Beth was a small woman who had not been capable of leaving her bed for almost a fortnight. She was torn inside and had lost a great deal of blood. She was little and skinny at the best of times, but just now she was nothing more than skin and bone, limping and slow-moving, exhausted. She could not explain how she had managed it; in fact, she couldn't remember the shed or the tin bath at all. What did she remember? Just that an awful feeling had come over her; that was all she could remember, an awful feeling.

And where were the babies during all this time? Had she left them upstairs while she went down into the yard to fetch the bath? Were they still lying in their crib in her bedroom, with Bert snoring just a few feet away on the bed? Or had she already brought them down, wrapped up, and left them lying together on the armchair in the scullery? She could only remember bringing them downstairs; after that, nothing.

Once filled up, the bath would have been far too heavy

for her to carry indoors to the warmth of the kitchen; was that why she had left it sitting under the tap of the rainwater butt that stood just outside the yard door? Perhaps she reasoned the fresh air would do them no harm. After all, it had been very hot that week, the house was stuffy, and the poor little mites had been cooped up indoors the whole time since the birth. But did she really think that cold rainwater would be suitable to wash two newborn babies in? Why not fetch the water in a kettle and boil it up on the stove and then bring the empty bath into the house and set it on the kitchen table before attempting to wash the twins? And why were they found still in their nightclothes? If it had been her intention simply to bath the babies, why had she kept their clothes on when she placed them in the water?

Oh, but she hadn't been thinking right. She was all of a muddle in her head. She just wasn't herself at all. Why, if she had been herself what happened next would never have happened at all: how could it have done?

If she had been herself she *never* would have thought to place the babies in the bath and then leave them there as the sunlight stretched across the yard, and the donkey shuffled in the old shed, and the birds opened their throats to greet the morning. She would *never* have left them there while she returned to the house, to lie in the bed listening before turning to shake Bert awake.

She could remember having heard a splash and the touch of cold water on her hands, but nothing else. She couldn't remember having felt anything until she turned to walk away. She thought she had heard the old donkey shuffle in the shed behind her as she went back into the house. She knew that as she climbed the stairs back to bed she'd felt lighter and everything had seemed clear all of a sudden, but she didn't know why. She had sort of floated up the stairs and everything had been peaceful and clear and she had slept deeply for the first time in weeks.

Then she must have woken up and remembered... something – she couldn't say what – "Bert! Bert! Go down and fetch the babies! I've left them downstairs!"

She had no idea why she would do such a thing. No idea whatsoever.

***

I am ten years old and spending time at the home of my mothers' parents, Reg and Ettie, while my mum is in hospital having a baby. Much as I love them, to me their home is depressingly dingy, fading, redolent with the smell of old clothes, boiled cabbage and lost dreams. There is nothing to do here except help my Nana with her knitting, bake scones, listen to the wireless and ask eternally for permission (rarely, if ever, granted) to go out on to the streets and play.

As a family, we are firmly set in the stratum that lies, as Johnson put it, "neither below mediocrity nor above it" (not a place to be for too long); we are "lower-middling", with pretensions, aspirations, and anxiety. There is anxiety both about reaching too high and about headlong falls into ruin and shame. There is anxiety about what other people might be thinking of us. Like all those others who spent the previous century clinging on somewhere near the lower-middle rung of the ladder, my family has done all it can to show the past in the best possible light. Anything distasteful, disreputable, unrespectable (you might even say anything interesting) has all been tidied away somewhere, like a toilet roll beneath a crocheted crinoline.

But every so often something so dreadful occurs in a family that the fear of it can never be entirely banished: it loiters in dark corners, it hovers overhead, and it manifests itself in the nervous tics, recurring nightmares and failed attempts at happiness of everyone whose blood-line it has tainted. At ten years old, I do not know what precisely the terrible, nameless thing that happened in my family is; all I know is that it happened a long time ago, before I was born, and yet it has never gone away. It is the ghost that haunts us.

When I see the ghost I am in my grandmother's tiny, steamy kitchen, sitting at the canary yellow Formica cabinet covered with black scrawlings (which looked just as if a spider had fallen into a pot of alcoholic ink and then gone for a walk across the surface). The cabinet is my grandmother's pride and joy, one of the few pieces of furniture she has ever bought "new", and it is apparently able to "clean itself". I am sitting there shelling peas into a colander and I can see the wedge of bills and correspondence from my grandfather's hat-making business, squashed up against the inside edge of the cabinet just above my eye-level, and the bottle of Daddies Sauce which is shoring them up. I hate the rictus of the black-and-white dad on the label, I hate his Brylcreemed head, and I hate his stupid enthusiasm for the revolting brown sauce my grandfather dollops over everything ("My favourite!").

On the stove my Nana has set mince and potatoes bubbling for our tea and the panlids are chattering excitedly. The smell of the mince mingles with a top note of Old Spice, as for some reason my grandfather prefers to shave each morning in the kitchen, even though my grandparents have a perfectly good bathroom. (It will be some years before I make the necessary calculations and realise that Reg did not live in a house with a bathroom until he left home, by which time he would have been well into his twenties. In fact, it is quite possible that he never had access to a bathroom until he and my grandmother moved into their house on the Camden Road, when he was in his mid-thirties. Old habits, as they say, die hard.)

My grandmother, Ettie, is standing by the stove, prodding the potatoes with a knife and telling me how to behave. "You'll need to help mummy when she is home with the baby, you know. You'll need to keep an eye on her." I shrug carelessly, and probably sneer as well, resentful that Nana feels the need to tell me. Don't need to be told, I think. I am always good and helpful, which is true, and besides I like babies. All girls like babies. But she is on a roll now and there is no stopping her. "Don't let mummy be alone too much with the baby, will you?" she goes on. "It's very important. Mummies can get a bit silly if they don't have enough rest after they've had a baby. And you girls will all have to watch out.....what with all that business with Reg's mother and all."

At this my ears prick up. What business with Reg's mother? The long-dead, somewhat shadowy person also referred to as my mother's "Grandma Wood"? An excellent cook, we are always told, so I imagine her resembling Mrs Bridges in TV's *Upstairs Downstairs*. Grandma Wood is also the individual charged by my Nana with spoiling my grandfather through "doting on him" far too much. He never talks about her, though. In fact, the atmosphere becomes strained whenever the conversation strays in the direction of his mother.

My grandmother is leaning on the stove to stir the mince. "What business, Nana?" I venture, innocently. Under my thumbs, the peas pop out of their pod and one or two of them spin around the colander.

"Oh, it was in all the newspapers... Reg's mother drowned her triplets and got sent to Broadmoor... She could have hanged... She'd still be there if the family hadn't got her out..."

Mad... Hanged... Broadmoor... Drowned... Triplets..? The daddy on the sauce bottle grins at me, and my heart pounds. What on earth can she *mean*?

It is just before half past five on the morning of Wednesday 27th August 1919. My grandfather (not yet my grandfather, still then young Reggie Wood with all his life ahead of him) is seventeen years old and beginning to stir. Barnet Fair starts on Monday and he has to help his dad prepare the blood horses, the trotters, they are hoping to sell either at the fair itself or on the way up. He has to do his work on the horses first thing, before Romford market sets up, because he also works there every Wednesday. The trotters are difficult to deal with because of their temperament: they require patience and a quiet firmness not many people possess. But the Wood men have a way with them, especially my grandfather who has a gentle, easy-going demeanour. And despite (or perhaps because of) the fact that this outward steadiness belies an intense inner life, the horses respond to him. Horses, dogs and children will respond positively to him his entire life.

He is going to help his dad with the horses because he is a good and dutiful son, one who loves both his parents, especially his mum, deeply and unquestioningly, but to tell the truth his heart is not really in it. He feels that "the horses" is not a particularly good line to be in and he is more than a little ashamed of it.

At seventeen Reg is desperate to go into a more respectable line of trade, an aspiration his mum encourages, conspiring with him, nudging him away from his dad and uncle and their diverse attempts at "business", most of it carried on with no more than sporadic success and (it must be said) dubious legality. For the past two or three years Reg has been working as a messenger for the millinery stall-holders in Romford market. He is by now quite thick with a number of them, and has earned a reputation as a hard-worker with a lot of personal charm. He is looking for an opening as a commercial traveller, and then he will buy himself a motor and have cards printed with his name on them.

With a heavy day's workload ahead of him, Reg is already awake when he hears his dad, Bert, on the landing outside the room he shares with his two little brothers, Stan, twelve, and Alfie, just three years old. It is possible that Reg's sleep had already been disturbed by some strange noise or other – perhaps the first indication that something is not quite right – though later he will report that he heard nothing until his dad called for him. This is somewhat strange in such a small house, but it is only one of a number of observations about that particular day which continue to perplex.

Bert is a big man, like an amiable ox. He takes care not to wake the two younger boys, as he leans into the room, his enormous frame filling the little doorway, and hisses my grandfather's name. "Reg, Reg. You awake boy?"

Thinking that it is time to start work, the boy leaves his bed, grabbing his heavy boots and pulling on his corduroy working trousers. When he comes out on to the landing, Bert seems smaller and somehow slower than usual, and looking at his dad, Reg can tell almost immediately that something is wrong. "You got to go call Mrs Bennett, boy," Bert whispers. Mrs Bennett is the local midwife (in fact just over seventeen years ago she had brought Reg himself into the world), and since the Saturday before last when Reg's mum, Beth, gave birth to triplets, Mrs Bennett has been a visitor to the house almost every day.

"Why?" he asks his dad. "What's happened?"

No sooner has he asked the question than it occurs to him that the house is very quiet, quieter than it has been for several days now. The landing is tiny, there is hardly enough room for Bert and him to stand there together without touching, and the top of the stairs is but one or two steps away from each of the three doors that surround it. Normally you can hear everything going on behind those doors, yet this morning there is no background chorus of cries coming from the other side of the door to his parents' room, no mewling and whimpering; there are no gurglings, splutterings, or little sucking noises. Nor can Reg hear his mum singing or chatting in her funny way…

"Is mum all right?" he asks. His dad is looking down at the floor. "Oh, Reg", he says, without looking up, "she's only been and drowned the babies…"

The two men do not touch. They do not move. The silence that follows is broken by a low groan from behind the door of his parent's room. A strange animal-like sound, as it etiolates into something more recognisably human, a feeble wail that extends into the dark space on the landing between Reg and his dad. It will hang there for the rest of their lives.

Reg puts on a terrible spurt: he covers the half-mile from his home on the London Road to Mrs Bennett's down in St Andrews in three minutes flat. When he arrives there it is still not much after a quarter to six. Mrs Bennett is only just waking up, so Reg has to spend ten minutes waiting for her in the kitchen. Her husband is a nice old boy, a local iron and metal dealer, well-known to the Woods as someone they can do a bit of business with (when the opportunity presents itself). He offers Reg a cup of tea, but this offer is politely declined. The friendly old man has known Reggie Wood since he was a baby, and has watched him grow into the gawky, distracted boy who now stands in the kitchen, struggling to retain his composure. Mr Bennett asks if there is anything he can do to help. He asks what's happened, but Reg tells him that he is very sorry, he can only talk about "it" to Mrs Bennett.

Who knows what words my grandfather (not yet my grandfather, then still a boy, desperate to do and say the right thing) chose in imparting his news to Mrs Bennett when she finally appeared in her kitchen? Whether he was blunt ("Mum has drowned the babies") or melodramatic ("Please come quick, Mrs Bennett. Something awful's happened...") – just how do you break that sort of news? Whatever it was he said, it was enough to ensure that the

28

midwife wasted no time in returning to the London Road house, which, in the half an hour or so since Reg left it, had become a scene of hysterical grief.

Mrs Bennett found Beth sitting up in bed, in a "very confused state", sobbing and wailing.

"Oh dear, Mrs Wood!" she exclaimed. "Whatever made you do this?" to which a "very excited and distressed" Beth replied, "Bert says I have drowned the babies, but I have *not*. I have only bathed them and left them downstairs."

My grandfather fades, for the time being, from the records, unless it was him who was sent to fetch Police Sergeant Wiseman and PC Bacon of the Romford constabulary. They arrived at the tiny terraced house at a quarter past six, where they found the babies, side by side and still fully-clothed, lying face upwards in a tin bath on the scullery table. It was probably one of the policemen who sent for the family doctor, George Cordy Jeaffreson.

Beth's first words to him, when he arrived at the house, at half-past seven, were: "Where are my babies?" He inspected the little bodies (he had not attended the confinement so had never seen them before) and pronounced them small, but well-developed, well-nourished and well cared for. He gave the cause of death in each case as suffocation by drowning and estimated that it would have taken approximately one-and-a-half minutes for them to die. Ninety seconds. That is all the time it takes...

By the end of that fateful morning Beth was in the Romford infirmary, seriously ill, and, in the words of the medical officer, "quite mentally unhinged". In her deluded state of mind she was probably the only member of the family unaware of what fate awaited her.

-2-

Grandma Wood

Mum can never talk about "Grandma Wood", her paternal grandmother, without smiling. She remembers a little cottage (like so much else, now gone) whose front stood at the very end of the Market Place in Romford, next to the loam pond and the old stocks and right behind the cattle scales. Through the lace-festooned windows nosy cows would often impertinently poke their snouts. They would have looked in on an immaculate, dainty abode, its tiny rooms suffused with needlework, handmade lace, patterned china, knick-knacks and the smell of baking. Mum remembers a back garden refulgent with the colour and scent of flowers, populated by huge bumble bees and giant butterflies, the branches of its fruit trees bedecked and overburdened with first blossoms and then sweet, juicy plums and apples and pears. She remembers chunky home-made jam spread thick on crusty home-made bread, pastry that melted in your mouth and at the heart of it all a tiny flame-haired grandmother, who was funny, spirited and kind.

Mum also remembers Grandma Wood at the end: how sad it was to see her become a confused old lady in a psychiatric ward, her once endearing dottiness declined into something more disturbing. And my mother can remember the day when she, as a twelve-year-old, made her own discovery of our family secret. She recalls coming across a newspaper cutting, or maybe a telegram – mum cannot remember which it was – referring in some congratulatory manner to the birth of triplets. Perhaps it was the item that appeared in the *Romford Times* issue of August 20th, 1919:

BIRTH OF TRIPLETS

Mrs Wood, wife of B W Wood of 18, London Road gave birth to triplets on Sunday morning. The infants were all girls and one of them died soon after birth. The other two and the mother are doing well. There are three other children in the family.

Had my great-grandmother kept it as a small reminder of her one brief moment of fame before her descent into infamy; as one solitary memento of her baby daughters? My mother remembers being confused by the discovery. "But you don't have triplets, Grandma…." she said. "No, dear, but I did," came the reply.

Later, back at home, my mother asked her parents about Grandma's triplets. My grandfather, rendered mute by the question, stood up and promptly left the room. It was not a subject she ever raised with him again.

I never knew Beth, my mother's "Grandma Wood", although I have her name as my middle name: the very first thing she and I have in common, apart from our ancestry. She died before I was born and so, for the longest time, to me she was only a figment of other people's memories, an indistinct figure in aging family photographs, and the author of a few letters written to my grandfather during the war in a scrawling hand that is very hard to read but which contains the essence of her voice as it was in life. I loved my grandfather and Beth loved him too, and that is the second thing which she and I have in common.

In the photos we have of her, Grandma Wood always looked to my childhood self as if she was made from pipe-cleaners: her spindly legs stretched out in front of her and crossed where they ended at her thin ankles, beyond which lay sensible sturdy black lace-ups which seemed too big for the rest of her. Little round specs were perched on her thin, beaky nose, but apart from them she was all angles and no curves. In the photos she is dressed in handmade floral print frocks, the sort that always used to be described as "cheerful", and often (even though all the snaps appear to have been taken on some summer picnic or other, or at the seaside) she is swathed in a heavy winter overcoat. Her hair sits on top of her little bony face like a big tuft of candy floss, and what you can't tell from the black and white photos is that it was dyed red.

In the photos Grandma Wood looks like a million other "old girls" who had lived through two world wars, with sad, hard lives behind them. These "old girls" had grown up in the shadow of the workhouse with the final indignity of a pauper's grave looming up in front of them. It was only through sheer hard work and determination that they managed to avoid both. They were dedicated to the eradication of dirt, deftly avoiding anything which would bring shame in all its many guises: dirty net curtains, unscrubbed front doorsteps, dusty knick-knacks, alcoholism, financial ruin, illegitimacy, unwanted pregnancy, madness... They used up their lives devising ever more ingenious ways to keep ruin at bay, scraping together pennies and pride. They slept with their purses underneath their pillows and eked out the contents with scrupulous care. They scrubbed and they swept and they polished and they rubbed.

Beth was relatively poor for most of her life and relatively powerless for all of it. She never had much of an education, or electric light, or a house with a bathroom or an indoor lavatory. Her principal abiding interest – her consuming passion – was "the family", but nobody ever knew how much she worried about them all. What they saw was a funny old thing bobbing about her little kitchen, baking cakes and making jam for them. She doled out love in thick ladles of custard and gravy, knitted and stitched it into socks and scarves and matinée jackets.

She wasn't one to leave herself out though. She was lively and chatty and she liked to keep up with what was going on. When she had to start her life over again, in the 1920s, a prematurely-aged forty-three-year-old, she dyed and bobbed her hair like the flappers. She made herself colourful dresses out of remnants bought at the market, and she made them fashionably short; so short, in fact, that when she bent down everyone could see her long flannel drawers and the tops of her lisle stockings. When she did her housework she liked to hum along to the romantic songs on the wireless (powered by an accumulator). And when she had a bit of time to herself she liked to sit at the kitchen table with a cup of tea and read the "stories" in her "story papers". Her gravely autodidactic eldest son dismissed them as "mill-girl literature", but although they clearly had different tastes in reading material, in all other respects they adored each other. She would rush into his arms when he came to visit (just like I did when a small girl) and he would lift her high in the air and twirl her about. "My Beth", he would cry, "my darling, darling Beth!"

Like all of us Beth had her secrets, and she had her dreams and her nightmares. Who knows what form those took? She always claimed never to remember the details of that summer night in 1919. She told the family, the police, the courts and the numerous clinicians who attended her that she could remember nothing at all between taking the twins downstairs and the moment she woke up and told Bert to go and fetch them. Nothing: it had all gone. But this was not entirely true. There were some memories, and how they haunted her. In those fading photographs taken on rare days off on the beach at Jaywick Sands, or while enjoying a picnic at Yardley Gobion, Beth is often captured with a faraway look in her eyes and a tired attempt at a smile on her lips.

My mother thinks it a great pity that Grandma Wood never saw television, because she would have really enjoyed following the soap operas – notwithstanding the fact that she had once figured prominently herself in events which could have provided the storyline for a dozen TV dramas.

***

I have been thinking about Beth and what she did for most of my life. Over the years I have been afraid of, if not her exactly, then the power of her deed. I have pitied her, I have tried to forget about her and push her to the back of my mind, and on occasion I have caught myself feeling ashamed of her, consciously deciding not to talk about her to certain people for fear of what conclusions they might draw about *me*. Beth's story has developed for me in layers, over the years, as I reached back through the past generations and forward from them to the present. For me, born three years after Beth died in a psychiatric hospital (then still widely referred to as the county "Lunatic Asylum"), this story begins with my mother – the only daughter of Beth's adored eldest son, Reg.

Grandparents and grandchildren can share a special

bond of unadulterated and unconditional love for one another, and so it was with my mother and Beth. Growing up, my mother only had one grandmother. Her mother's mother, Nel – by popular consent a beautiful and sweet-natured woman who left her remote home on the foothills of Snowdonia to follow her soldier sweetheart far away from their native Wales, bore nine healthy children and lost a handful more – was worn out at forty-four ("too good to live", everyone said) and she died young, eighteen years before my mother was born.

My mother's mother (Ettie, Nel's third child) never recovered from the loss. Sixty years later she could still weep bitterly at the memory of her mother's sudden passing, displaying a grief every bit as intense as if it had happened just a few days ago. Ettie was insecure and vulnerable to the point of instability and, like many people who have to give much of their attention over to keeping feelings in check, she was capable of great insensitivity to others, often saying the first thing that came into her head with devastating results. As a mother, she swung between unbounded adulation and smarting criticism, and as a result the relationship my mother had with her could be combustible, overwhelming: it was full of love, but it was far from easy.

In the absence of any other contenders, Grandma Wood provided my mother with an alternative, indulgent mother figure. In her home mum found a cosy haven, a place where nobody would expect her to be anything other than she was. And Beth, the mother of sons, took delight in passing on to my mother, her only surviving female descendent, all the things she believed a woman should know about: everything from periods to pancakes. It was her standards of homeliness, neatness and unqualified affection to which my mother aspired.

Looking back now, mum says she finds it ironic to say the least that a woman convicted of drowning two of her newborn babies should have been the main conduit through which lessons about being a wife and mother flowed from the past to the present, but that was really how it was. These days when my mother looks in the mirror she says that it is Beth's image she sees looking back, an observation tinged with sadness, around which an unvoiced concern echoes. When mum says that she is "turning into" her Grandma she also hints that she is a little perturbed by the transformation. Grandma Wood, whatever else she may or may not have been, was "difficult", "awkward" and "quite mad", and my family, even after all this time, is afraid of that madness.

**

For years when my grandfather was still alive we were not allowed to talk about "it" at all, and now when we can talk about "it" we do so only within bounds set every bit as firmly. We do not dare to consider the actual circumstances of that event, only those aspects which chime in with our

sympathetic rendition. We do not speculate on the foren-
sic aspect, the physical process she followed through, the
act itself. We do not doubt that Grandma Wood was "out
of it", "unaware", "completely doolally" at the time, but
we never admit the possibility that perhaps she simply
wanted to "get rid of" her twin girls. We make excuses for
her: she did not "murder" her babies, we say, she "did not
know what she was doing". Our retelling of this chapter in
Beth's life is a process of emendation which began on the
day itself, more than eighty years ago. We have yet to accept
that Beth really did drown her newborn daughters in cold
rainwater, yet she never denied that she did that, so why
do we? Beth, we say, had "suffered so much", she was "not
really to blame". The way we tell it, Beth was not really
there at all when her babies were drowned.

And for many years we did not even think about the
babies. We knew nothing about them, apart from the fact
that they were drowned. We thought there were three of
them and that they were boys.

Then one of us has her own baby and the previously
unthinkable thought comes crashing into our consciousness, sits itself down and obdurately refuses to budge: is
there any danger that I could do what *she* did?

Memory is always a casualty of trauma, but not
because shock obliterates the process of remembering. Far
from it: the details of calamitous events are carved deep
into the surface of the brain, and however hard they try the
victims of trauma cannot ever completely efface them.

They become a part of what de Quincey called the "palimpsest of indestructible memories" which give us form and shape. If ever we succeed in pushing the memory back into storage, it will seep into our dreams and implicate itself upon other aspects of our waking life. Ultimately, I suppose de Quincey is right: it is our traumas which make us who we are, and the ghostly adumbrations of long-past traumas which are our true inheritance.

**

My maternal grandfather, Reg, was charming, bookish, endlessly patient and very gentle. And I adored him. I still derive enormous pleasure from telling myself that I am his favourite – even though he has been dead for over twenty-five years. But Reg was also bitterly disappointed by life and he carried a deep sorrow, always there, in his sad brown eyes. It gave him a vulnerable appeal which I am sure was not lost on the numerous women he successfully wooed.

Reg was a very natty fellow, always turned out smartly in a jacket, shirt and tie, knitted waistcoat, his brogues polished to a mirror shine. He was never seen without his trilby hat, which out of doors only came off to salute a passing hearse or a lady. He was faultlessly well-mannered, but he never could shake off his awareness that he was not a true gentleman, just a "gent". He was ashamed that he had received no formal education past the age of eleven and he would visit the library every Friday evening as soon as he finished work, carefully choosing four volumes (history, biography and Charles Dickens mostly) which he then sat and read all weekend. It was as if he was trying to cram as much knowledge as possible into his head before it was too late. He was well-respected by the people he did business with, local tradesmen and the rough "costers" who lived in the area around London Bridge, where he worked for many years. To all of them he was a scholar, an urbane dispenser of wisdom, but the approbation of others meant little to him. What he really wanted was to live up to his own expectations of himself.

Until the late 1940s he had, in his unintentionally comic parlance (he never joked about hats), "travelled in ladies' millinery", and at some point he had had a big showroom on the corner of Oxford Circus and Great Portland Street in the West End. He dealt with such doyens of the trade as Christopher of Hove and supplied all the big stores. The war was a boom period for millinery, as hats were off the clothing ration, but after the war "the Queen" (I am guessing it was the old Queen Mum, but it might have been the then Princess Elizabeth) started turning up places wearing a headscarf, and the bottom dropped right out of the hat business. As a consequence, Reg was condemned to spend the next (actually the last) twenty-five years of his life making seaside novelty hats in a cramped, stiflingly hot, noxious workshop under the railway arches in Flat Iron Square, Southwark, which shook violently each time the trains rumbled overhead on their way to and from London Bridge station. The shop resembled a medieval chamber of horrors with its vats of boiling hot liquid, the hydraulic blocking machine and huge tongs and trimming irons, all of which looked like torture instruments. Felt-hat-making is dirty, hard work. My grandfather manufactured the felt himself from rags, bought by the ton, which sat in mountainous heaps in a cellar beneath the workshop. The cellar smelt of death and the river.

The conditions in which he worked were grim and primitive, yet my grandfather retained an invincible core of pride in his craft, hand-blocking and hand-finishing each Kiss Me Quick, Cowboy and PC99 with as much care and precision as he must once have spent on his fancy *chapeaux* – the postillions in amber felt, trimmed with turquoise lace, the black felt halos bedecked with red ostrich plumes. His once beautifully manicured nails were cracked and stained black from the stiffener and dyes that bubbled away in the huge cauldrons in the middle of the shop-floor: a permanent reminder of how far he had sunk. Yet woe betide anyone bold enough to tell him that he was "mad" to take so much trouble over the hats when the buyers would have been happier with something far less perfect. "What's the point of doing something unless you do it properly?" he would rage. "You might as well chuck the whole bloody lot in and stay in bed for the rest of your bloody life." Sometimes it did seem he would do that.

Although to me my grandfather was a great stump of

oak, I can see now that he was, in essence, rootless. He was given to fugue: disappearing for weeks at a time when a young man, leaving my grandmother to cope alone with the children – and the bills. She never lost the habit of worrying about where he was and what he was up to, even though by the time I knew him, when he was old, he had stopped physically running away. By then he would fall instead into sudden and intractable silences, or lie in his bed for the whole of a day. These were times when he really did seem to be detached from the rest of us.

In striking contrast to my grandmother Ettie (who boasted a vast clan of siblings and cousins and their spouses and children, and who claimed kinship with every other Welsh person she encountered), Reg appeared to have only his wife, his son and daughter and his grandchildren in the world. In some ways it was as if his life began the day he married my grandmother. There was no contact with his two younger brothers or any of what was actually a vast network of cousins. He very rarely talked about his aunts, uncles or grandparents.

He dealt out the story of his life in little portions of well-rehearsed anecdotage. The entertaining tales he told about himself – never told quite the same way twice – were really just so much patter designed to amuse, but also to obfuscate: they were part of a verbal sleight of hand every bit as skilful as that he employed when magicking pennies from behind my ears. He had a couple of jolly tales about his dad – mostly to do with the old boy's prodigious strength and knowledge of horses, and the way Bert and his brother had cobbled antiques in the 1920s. But he had very little to say about his mum, and I can remember only one occasion when he mentioned by name his little sister, Maisie, who had died aged four when Reg was in his mid-teens.

I spent countless days in my grandfather's company through all the years I was growing up, and yet most of what I know about him came to me second-hand. Often if you asked him a direct question about his past he would pretend he hadn't heard; if you persisted he would simply withdraw himself from the conversation. It was so horrible to be rejected by him, to be banished from his favours and his usual kindly interest, that after a while one learnt simply never to ask. Why, I used to wonder, did he always have to keep his distance? What was he hiding? Once, only once, he let me in on a secret. He showed me the red and blue star he had tattooed on the inside of his left wrist. He told me that a gypsy at a fair (both gypsies and fairs figured strongly in his life) had given it to him when he was a boy of eleven or twelve. It was, he said in deadly earnest, one of the biggest regrets of his whole life. When he arrived back home thus defaced his mother had burst into a terrible and wholly uncharacteristic rage. She had railed at him, told him that now he would never amount to anything, that his life was finished: and then, fury spent, she had sobbed inconsolably for what seemed like hours.

This is the only time I can ever remember my grandfather telling me a story about Beth. She emerges from it as relentless – harsh even – in her urge for progress, yet there is also something desperate in her determination to avoid ruin. On that day Beth made my grandfather feel so ashamed that for the rest of his life he kept the tattoo hidden, developing a nervous tic that required him unconsciously, to pull down his shirt cuff whenever he thought the little blue and red star might be visible. It was as though the "commonness" his family was so anxious to avoid was branded upon him.

Ironically, however, it was Beth who was to be the source of an even deeper shame, the disseminator of a sadness that trammelled my grandfather and shaped his mind for depression and failure. The act of destruction that morning when she drowned his two baby sisters was, in itself, bad enough – but the terrible shame, the stamp of madness and the stigma of having a convicted murderess for a mother would all prove to be far more enduring than anything a fairground gypsy could accomplish with a pin and a bottle of India ink.

I knew that the subject of his mother was definitely on the "forbidden" list, and the last thing I wanted was to drive my grandfather off on one of his flights. But once, just once, desperate for some sort of explanation or reassurance, I broached the subject with him. He spun round and shouted his words into my face like a slap: "What do you want to drag all *that* up for?" he demanded. "What do you want to drag all that up for?" It is the only time I can ever remember him being angry with me.

***

By the time, years later, that I was ready to confront my fears about the past, it was to the past I turned for guidance. By then my grandparents were all dead and I suppose I had become more keenly aware of connections and disconnection as I made my own way in the world, with two little boys to teach and prepare for the future. Maybe I wanted to help root them, in order to keep them here, with me, as long as possible; maybe, too, I wanted to invoke the ancestral gods to help me keep them safe, to break the Ju-ju curse.

When in 1997 after the birth of my second son I started my weekly journeys to the Family Record Centre in Islington, north London, to investigate my grandfather's family, I had a tremendous sense of purpose. I needed to find out the truth for so many reasons, and I also wanted to give dimension and a human face to my great-grandmother Beth, to somehow bring back to life her twin daughters, the sisters and aunts lost forever to my mother's family. George Eliot put it far more eloquently than I ever could when she wrote in *Middlemarch* of her intention to "show the gradual action of ordinary causes rather than exception..." I wanted to see whether or not something as exceptional as infanticide is in fact mired in the mundane, the quotidian and, by so doing, whether or not it is understandable, or even believable. Perhaps, I reasoned, if I could succeed in delineating the ordinary trajectory of my great-grandmother's life, I would be able to comprehend the extraordinary tangent it had taken. And if I could do that, then, maybe, so could others.

The arrival of a baby is a psychological adventure: it pushes a woman back into memories of her own babyhood, back into collective memories of parenting and back into the animal, instinctual part of her being. It urges her to confront her relationship with her own mother and, in no small way, all the mothers in her line. When she gives birth for the first time a woman is herself reborn: she sheds the protective layers of selfhood built up over the entire course of her life; she has to confront her own fears of pain and death; and she must forge an entirely new relationship with the outside world. She is no longer somebody's child, but somebody's mother.

Giving birth for the first time, in 1985, was the most traumatic experience of my life to date. Almost from the moment I arrived at the hospital on a bright autumnal day, a healthy, happy young woman, things started to go horribly wrong. I was already in labour, and suffering strong lower back pains. During the course of routine examinations it was discovered that something was not as it should be. The obstetrician was summoned, and he told me that my baby was "transverse lie". "How on earth did that happen?" he kept asking nobody in particular. I mumbled an apology, thinking that whatever it was it must have been something I had done. I was sent for a scan to make sure, and it transpired that not only was my baby lying across my womb, with his head lodged under my left ribs and his bottom under my right, he was also quite large and there was some indication of "cephalopelvic disproportion". The obstetrician drew me a diagram: even if they were able to manipulate my baby into a more acceptable presentation (a "frank breech", say, enabling them to pull him out bottom first, or even a "footling breech", in which case my son would enter the world by one foot at a time), the fact that my pelvis was so small meant that I would need something they kept calling "a C-section".

I was woefully ignorant. In the first flush of enthusiasm for the big adventure of pregnancy I had bought a book about giving birth, but only because it was full of beautiful images suffused with the orange glow of the foetal universe. I had skipped over the "difficult" bits in the leaflets handed out at antenatal, assuming that they would never apply to me. The video they showed in the waiting-room, as I sat there with all the other pregnant women clutching my still warm sample of pee, consisted of a head and shoulders shot of a panting and sweating woman who could have been opening an especially obstinate pickle jar for all anyone could see. Besides it always ended with happy tears and a darling baby wrapped in spotless cotton, so who cared about the preamble? I had been very good about attending my mothercraft classes, even though I was usually the only mum-to-be who came there on her own (my husband at the time was always working away from home), and hated having to do my breathing exercises with the physiotherapist squeezing my toes rather than my birth-partner. I had written a birth-plan during my ante-natal appointments, airily requesting that pain relief only be given to me if I asked for it. I had bought myself a bottle of eau de Cologne and a large nursing bra with zips under the cups: I thought I was all set. I can honestly say that I had absolutely no idea what the obstetrician was talking about.

As the midwives and student 'gynies' gathered around me to witness the medical anomaly I had become ("Do you mind – only it's probably the only time they will get to see a transverse lie and CPD?"), I innocently asked whether I would be allowed to listen to the tape of soothing music I had made, while I delivered my baby. In the embarrassed, ensuing silence, the midwife quietly explained that I would be giving birth in theatre. That was when I realised that C-Section stood for caesarean. I went into shock. I burst out crying. But my mother never had any trouble having babies, I argued feebly. As I signed the consent form I tried to console myself: I had been secretly worried about whether I could deal with pain; I had scared myself wondering how a baby's head could possibly pass through something as small and narrow as a vagina; I was afraid of being left stretched and torn and unattractive to my husband. Now I told myself I had no more need for hidden anxieties: my body had decided for me. I was not made for childbirth; I was too small; I did not have childbearing hips after all, but the realisation only made me feel a sad failure, unwomanly. As I was being prepared for the anaesthetic I made a joke about not being able to wear a bikini again. The doctor made a joke of his own about how I would still be able to keep a "tight grip" on my man.

In the recovery room after the operation, the birth of my first child, I suffered a massive haemorrhage and I almost died. It was in the early days of the HIV scare, late on a Friday afternoon, and I have a rare blood group: three pieces of bad luck which meant I could not have a transfusion until the haematology staff returned from their weekend off. I suffered another haemorrhage when back on the ward a little while later and became severely anaemic. By then I was also physically and emotionally traumatised, exhausted and, of course, suffering all the usual aftermath associated with major abdominal surgery (catheter, morphine drip, pain, immobility). And I also had a newborn baby to love and keep alive. For days I was unable to do little more than drift in and out of consciousness, barely aware most of the time where I was.

Confusion and helplessness overtook me, and I was to feel that way, on and off, for most of the next six months. I could not believe that I had come into the hospital a healthy young woman, and would be leaving ten days later, defeated, a bloodless wreck. I had enormous unvoiced anxiety about everything that had happened to me: why had I needed a caesarean; why had I lost so much blood; what had happened to my baby while I was being revived and my husband was pacing the corridor outside the operating theatre? And I wondered why nobody seemed to understand how hard it was for me to look after my baby when I had just endured major surgery with complications a few days before. I felt too ashamed to ask these questions, when it seemed as if I was the only woman on the earth who had ever felt that way, the only woman on earth who was not designed for natural childbirth.

It took me a long time to recover. For the first six months of my son's life, I was very depressed, extremely agitated, unable to settle to anything or to concentrate. I was constantly fidgety and butterflies continually fluttered about in my stomach. I would be changing or feeding the baby or washing his clothes and all the while my foot would be tapping or my fist clenching and unclenching and I would be saying under my breath "Come on, come on". Interspersed with this hyperactivity were bouts of overwhelming fatigue. I drove myself on until I had blinding headaches from the voices in my head which by turns encouraged and then derided my efforts. I would put my baby in his pram and walk for miles, anywhere, just walking and walking and walking and talking, talking, talking to him, to myself. I was striated with self-pity yet unable to do anything to help myself.

For years afterwards I suffered from nightmares and flashbacks, and even after all this time I still have a deep-rooted fear of doctors and hospitals. In one recurring dream I found myself in a cavern in which mothers stood around rock pools watching their babies drown. The mothers were entirely passive, looking on but without really seeing. They did not appear to feel any emotion. Sometimes nurses in starched white uniforms and thick white crepe-soled shoes would step in, but only to hold a little head under the water to ensure that death came more quickly. The fat, shiny, dimpled bodies of the drowned babies slipped along the bevelled surface of a metal sluice before vanishing into a great swirling lock. In the dream I ran about desperately trying to save the babies, scooping them out of the pool in armfuls, but they were slippery and would drop back into the water. I would run around the other mothers imploring them to help me, and they just nodded back at me, smiling and uncomprehending.

But most nights, that first half-year of motherhood, I lay awake, exhausted yet unable to sleep, convinced that something awful was going to happen to my baby and in despair at the recurring fear that the something awful might be me. It was as if I did not dare trust my sleeping self. There was a good reason why. One night, when I was still in the hospital, roaming the hinterland nursing mothers inhabit in the time between bouts of fitful sleep and the first hungry cry of the day, I had a terrifying thought.

What if, I reasoned, I was to place my pillow over my baby's face? Surely then all my troubles would be over? No sooner had I thought the previously unthinkable than pure relief surged through me: relief that there was, after all, a way out of this circle of Hell I found myself in, and relief that I was after all able to take back control over my own life and restore everything to pre-birth normality. Above all I was relieved that I would no longer be "a mother", but could become "me" again. Almost immediately (and this entire thought process must have occurred within a split second) I was filled with an overwhelming, insurmountable desire to protect my son. I knew in an instant that there was nothing I would not do in order to safeguard this little person lying in his crib by the side of my bed. Within a flickering moment I had crossed a line: I had become truly mad, able to rationalise the most heinous deed and, for some reason, just as quickly, I had crossed back again.

I suppose, looking back, I teetered on the brink of madness throughout this entire period of transition but, for some reason, I never went over the edge. I measured this – still do – by the fact that I never considered killing myself, although I did often think of never waking up again. There were certainly occasions when I resented my son for taking away my right to kill myself, but I accepted that my primary responsibility was now to this other person, my constant companion in that treacherous journey from girlhood to womanhood and from womanhood to motherhood.

It was unbearable to think, after all that he and I had been through together, that I could lose him through my own carelessness or stupidity. This worry tormented me all through the days and nights. The effort of staying with the task of keeping him alive took every iota of my strength. I felt childlike, useless and immature; I wanted my mother to come and rescue me from this mess I had put myself in. I was trying so hard and yet failing so thoroughly at something so important.

Needless to say, in due course I convinced myself that all my deficiencies and my incipient insanity were the inevitable consequence of inheriting the "bad mother gene" from Beth. This gave me an odd sort of comfort as all such handy explanations tend to do, but it also kept me away from anyone who might otherwise have helped me because, I reasoned, the fact of my despair had to be concealed at all costs from the doctors and health visitors. If I so much as asked for help, the "truth" about me would be out they would haul me off to a psychiatric ward and I would lose my beloved baby to the social services. The dark terror of "discovery" became an obsession. I became panicky whenever I had to visit the doctor with my baby, fearful that I would make some disclosure revealing my "true" self. Worse, I seemed to transmit my terror to my son who normally placid and happy would begin to scream as soon as we entered the clinic. This only made me feel even more of a failure: an unfit mother, who did not deserve the wonderful gift of a healthy child.

In fact as I learned much later, my fears were not without some basis. As one standard guide to new mothers puts it: "The more severe the bout of postnatal depression (PND), the more likely it is that the origins could be hereditary." There are plenty of statistical analyses which purport to prove that women who come from families (like mine) with a history of psychiatric illness are up to eighty per cent more likely to suffer a severe episode of post-partum psychosis than are others. And it is hardly comforting to learn that once you have suffered one episode of post-partum depressive illness most experts believe that you have up to a fifty per cent chance of a recurrence in your subsequent pregnancies.

This body of opinion left me extremely anxious about having any more children, and when I did finally fall pregnant for the second time, eleven years later, I was careful not to "prejudice" the doctors and midwives against me and kept quiet about my earlier experiences, in particular my brush with "madness". I was still very afraid that any such disclosure would lead to "them" taking my children away from me. The thought of that happening terrified me. For however much I felt I was unable to cope with the demands my sons made of me I was in no doubt that my life's task lay solely in protecting them.

It is so strange for me to look back on this time – all these years later – and see that in a few moments, back on that maternity ward, almost imperceptibly I had transformed from the archetypal "cruel mother", one who coldly contemplates smothering her baby with a pillow in order to preserve her own identity, to the archetypal "good mother", one who places the survival of her baby above everything else, including her own psychological survival. Or am I, in fact, an "overprotective" mother, one who loves "too much", and in danger of smothering my sons not with a pillow, but with my palpable anxiety?

Even now after all these years of practice I still find the enterprise fraught with self-doubt. Controversial recent diagnoses of Münchausen's Syndrome by Proxy, where mothers convince doctors that their children need often traumatic, invasive treatments for illnesses that are allegedly entirely the product of delusion, has made it even more difficult to draw the line between unconditional "mother love" and what has been called "smother love". To some extent obsessive love – over-voiced concern, deep-rooted maternal anxiety about the ability of your child to survive – can now all be construed as a form of abuse. Yet, now as ever, the entanglements of families, the webs of guilt and selfish desire, resentment and love continue to seem perfectly natural to those caught in their snare. Just how, exactly, does one "mother"? Is there a "right" or "wrong" way?

For my own part, life with my sons has taught me that it is necessary to take a big step back from my own preoccupations and obsessions. I have learnt, I continue to learn, that it is possible, for example, to both love and resent at the same time, that the up-down, back-and-forth swing between the two is part of the essential rhythm of life, that both emotions are equally overwhelming and heartbreaking; that the entire process is mysterious and unfathomable. And I have long since learnt to accept the incubus of anxiety that descends to sit on my heart in the middle of the night. In fact it is now impossible for me to imagine living the rest of my life without this terrible burden, this obsessive fear that something will happen to take my precious tormentors away from me. In short, of course, I cannot imagine life without them.

And so it must have been with Beth.

-3-

"Pity the poor cobbler who crouches in a stall under a house in some narrow street..."

It was said that all a master shoemaker needed to set himself up in business was a room and a five pound note, and even though the pages of the *Boot and Shoe Reporter* were already beginning to fill up with bankruptcy notices, Joe Smith, like his father and grandfather before him, a master bootmaker, decided he had nothing to lose by leaving his home village and setting himself up in a town. So it was that sometime in 1874 he put his kit on his back and, with his wife Lou and the two youngsters in tow (the boy, Herbert, aged four, and one-year-old Julia), set off to walk sixty-five miles across the entire breadth of Northamptonshire, to the town of Tamworth.

The move to Tamworth was probably the most daring thing Joe and Lou ever contemplated doing. They had lived all their lives in the same cluster of small villages, each consisting of no more than a couple of thousand inhabitants, where every other cottage contained a relative. The couple were in their early thirties, and yet in all probability had rarely, if ever, ventured much beyond a ten-mile radius of home. A visit to the races at Towcester, five miles to the north, or to the market at Stony Stratford, three miles to the south, would have constituted big trips for them and their families, taking them far enough beyond their narrow horizons.

Tamworth in the 1870s was a sizeable town, with a population of about five thousand, but it was far smaller and much less industrial than either Coventry or Birmingham and was therefore a wise choice (always assuming that there was a choice in the matter) for two naïve country people trying to make their way in the world. Contemporary descriptions of Tamworth paint a pleasing picture: a clean place, with a picturesque castle, and surrounded by lush meadows through which coursed the town's two rivers, the Tame and the Anker. The Birmingham and Derby Junction Railway had reached the town in the 1850s, and the Anker Viaduct, with its eighteen arches, rose more than twenty feet above the river, but this was considered more a thrilling spectacle than an eyesore. It was beneath its vaulting arches, at 59 Bole Bridge Street, on 4th September 1878, that Beth, Joe and Lou's fourth child, was born.

The lives of poor country-dwellers, like Beth's mum and dad, in the nineteenth century, were wretched for the most part, but they knew how to survive. They trusted that the land would provide wild berries and hedgerow fruits, pecks of grain missed by the threshers and the occasional poached rabbit. They were not prepared for the shock of being pushed into factories and towns. The "peasant poet" John Clare (1793-1864) came from the same wooded part of Northamptonshire as they did, a region once entirely protected by a great, dense forest, and he chronicled the loss of the woodland, and how it affected the local people. In his verse, he evoked the "smothered sigh" of the poor, a sigh still discernible today, as it heaves down through the generations of dispossessed.

Joe – just like his father, grandfather and great-grand-father before him – had been apprenticed to a cordwainer (or master shoemaker) in 1855, at the age of thirteen. By then Northamptonshire had been the centre of shoemak-ing in England for over two hundred years, thanks to its natural advantages: a plentiful supply of oak bark provid-ing charcoal necessary for the leather tanning process, and extensive grass plains stretching across the county from Warwickshire to East Anglia, and filled with enough cattle hide for all the shoes in England.

Joe came from the pretty village of Wicken, where he had grown up in the cottage home of his mother's parents – an agricultural labourer and a lace-maker, typical of the great majority of their neighbours and relations, and, like Clare, part of the great English tradition of ballad and song (Clare's own father, an illiterate flail thresher, was able to sing over one hundred ballads from memory). Even though they were relatively poor and humble, Joe's mother's family have left a strong trace in the village: their bell-ringing and choral-singing skills are commemorated on numerous plaques inside Wicken church, and their names appear on several gravestones in the churchyard. But the three-roomed cottage where Joe grew up, next door to the village pub, has long since gone, its site now occupied by a carpark.

By the time Beth was born in 1878, Joe was a master bootmaker and in his twenty-three years enjoined to the trade he would have witnessed more changes than his forefathers had seen in generations. The first sewing-machines, designed to sew the leather parts of the upper together, were brought to Kettering, centre of the Northamptonshire trade, from America in 1856 during the first year of Joe's apprenticeship, an event which prompted a strike (shoemakers had a long tradition of political radicalism). Most cordwainers refused to believe that the machine shoes would ever replace the hand-crafted shoes they made. But over the course of Joe's life each hand operation of the shoe-making process was gradually replaced by a machine, and thousands of village shoe and bootmakers abandoned their own shops and went into the factories which were spreading across the shoemaking centres of England, there to turn out cheap and durable mass-produced footwear.

Joe, then, was part of a dying breed. But he was also proud and determined (or perhaps stubborn and stupid) for he never stopped making shoes in the way he had been taught to do. Until his death in 1899 he struggled to maintain his independent status and never went to work in a factory. No doubt he was disparaging of the modern factory boots with their India-rubber soles, which were made to fit approximately, not precisely. He would have had no time for the sewing, blocking, riveting and pegging machines, and he would have bemoaned the general decline in status and respect afforded to craftsmen such as himself. Shoemakers were part of the artisanal aristocracy, inducted into the mysteries of their trade by dint of long family ties. It would take more than a few machines to wear them down. Of course, in the end that is precisely all it took.

By the time Beth's older brother took his place at the cobbler's bench towards the end of the nineteenth century, the gentle craft had been utterly diminished. The last shoemaker in my grandfather's lineage worked as a shoe-riveter, part of a cottage production line with all his near neighbours similarly employed in different parts of the complex shoemaking process. In 1901 he and his neighbours in the Northamptonshire village of Raunds could all be found out-finishing army boots for the Boer War. But, by 1913, the trade was already considered quaint enough for a lifesize model of a "cobbler's shop" to be included in Northampton Museum, in an early example of Heritage Britain. There was a brief respite granted to the trade in World War One, when Northamptonshire makers were needed once more to make the fifty million pairs of army boots required for the Front. But that upturn was short-lived. By the outbreak of World War Two, the village shoemaker was entirely a thing of the distant past.

Like most shoemakers, Joe, his father and his paternal grandfather were literate men – something which marked them out from the majority of their class. An etching from the 1820s entitled *The Village Politician* depicts a bespectacled shoemaker perusing a pamphlet as he takes a break from his work. Victorian shoemakers were generally considered – and no doubt considered themselves – to be a cut above the hoi polloi, and this is how I see Beth's dad, Joe. The trade he plied not only provided a necessary commodity, it required a good eye, sensitivity to shape, form and material, a steady hand and the intelligent mastery of an array of skills. I can discern the adumbration of Joe in my own stubborn, proud, bookish and infinitely painstaking grandfather, as he stood in the middle of those towers of Kiss Me Quick hats, each one made with punctilious attention to detail, even though it would only put a few coppers in his pocket. Like my grandfather after him, Joe derived a great deal of his sense of self from his status as an independent tradesman: one who proudly ticked the box on the census form which inquired if one were "neither employee nor employer", but "working on own account". Many would say about Joe, as they would later say of his grandson, that he was a stubborn old fool, but he was always his own man. It seems he never went cap in hand to the factories in Kettering in search of an "occasion", and he certainly never went "on the parish", no matter how bad things were.

The agrarian depression of the 1870s utterly defeated many of his class and type, but not Joe. In Northamptonshire and Buckinghamshire, as elsewhere, wheat prices fell dramati-cally and unemployment among farm labourers was very high. Stuck in a rural backwater as Joe was, with a local population who were now so impoverished they could hardly afford to have their boots mended, let alone replaced with a new pair, Joe became even more dependent than usual on the local area factors – the dealers, who sold on his wares to retail outlets. When demand was high, after the extra harvest payments, for instance, when entire families would pitch up at his door asking for their annual pair of new boots, Joe could take or leave the extra orders coming in from the factor. But during pinch times his relationship with them, if he was anything like his grandson, would have tilted much too far in their favour for his liking.

It did not take Joe long to figure out that there was little reason to stay put, and for a while he transplanted himself, his wife and his little son to Deanshanger, next door to Wicken. This was a smart move: the Buckingham arm of the Grand Union Canal had cut through Deanshanger in 1801, and this, coupled with its proximity to the Oxford road, had transformed the village into the nearest approximation the area had to an industrial centre. A large and successful iron foundry business had been established in the 1820s, which, in its heyday, regularly employed over a hundred men, who must have needed new boots from time to time. However, Joe still felt he could do better for himself and his growing family (the couple's first daughter, Julia, was born in Deanshanger in 1873). Hence the move to Tamworth.

It was not long before Joe would have to admit that he had probably overreached himself in making this move. He was not a good enough business man to overcome the odds stacked against him, and it was difficult for the family to survive, cut off as they were from the support networks they had always been used to. Being so far from home must have taken its toll on Lou, in particular, who by 1881 had five young children to look after in addition to helping Joe in the business. The couple had sent their second daughter, Martha, back home to live with Lou's parents in the Buckinghamshire countryside by the time she was six years old, which parents often did when a child was thought too sickly to survive in towns and cities, and it might well have been an additional source of stress for Lou, to be so far away from a "waukly" child. She may have been worried, too, about her aged parents, already beginning their distressing slide into pauperism. Whatever the reason, within a decade Beth's family were heading back to Northamptonshire – a somewhat humiliating return to the country which provided the first taste of failure for the couple, a taste with which they would become all too familiar.

Potterspury is set in pretty countryside, which looks much hillier than it actually is. It is situated three miles north of the roundabouts, concrete cows and shopping malls of Milton Keynes New Town, but in the 1880s it was one of the few sites of occupation in the heart of a largely uninhabited landscape. It was here that Joe now set himself up as the village shoemaker. And from the time she was five Beth always thought of this place as "home". The little three-roomed cottage in which the family lived fronted on to Watling Street, the great Roman road which cuts a swathe from Dover to Holyhead in north Wales, the gateway to Ireland, now known more prosaically as the A5.

As an old woman Beth, who otherwise kept herself to herself and bustled through the town avoiding contact with others, liked to look out of her cottage window onto the bustle of Romford market, observing, taking pleasure from the activities of others, but never fully participating. Was this a habit acquired as a child on Watling Street? Did she like to watch the steady stream of riders and coaches passing through and occasionally stopping off at the Old Talbot inn next door? Did she wonder where they had come from and where they were going to? Did she ever wish that they would take her with them as the thrum of their horses' hooves and the trundle of their cart wheels caused the little windows of her childhood home to rattle, the foundations to tremble?

Beth grew up not so much over as actually in her father's workshop, which occupied a portion of the ground-floor room of the family home. In addition to this room there was a tiny scullery containing a small fire grate with a little oven, and a tank at one side to heat the water which was fetched in from a standpipe in the lane outside. Upstairs there were two bedrooms, one for the children (six of them by 1885) and one for the parents.

Joe spent a large part of every day bent over his wooden lasts, covered with the leather shapes which the clicker – the skilled outworker who cut the hide – had brought by. The last was held in place on his left thigh by means of a stirrup which passed underneath his foot, and which he kept taut as he stitched the lasted insole and the upper to the welt. He darted threads left and right, in and out of a series of neat punch-holes he had made with his thick square awl in the layers of stiffened leather, and then in one deft movement pulled them through as tight as possible. As he pulled each stitch through, Joe would extend his arms out to his sides, holding aloft ends of the threads of waxed hemp or flax in each hand. This he would do hundreds and hundreds of times a day, nipping the threads with his thumb and forefinger each time, to complete the stitch.

Once the shoe was assembled he would turn his attention to building up the heel, in layers of leather, riveted together before being burnished with a hot glazing iron. Finally the leather would be "sleeked" with a long stick, smoothing out the wrinkles, before being buffed to a high polish.

Even without the encumbrances of Joe's business, the family home would have been a cramped, smoky, poorly ventilated and ill-lit space. The smell of burnished leather would have permeated every part of it and it would have resounded with the hiss of glazing irons set in coal brassieres and the rip of hemp threads being pulled through leather. I can imagine a little of what it must have been like, because it was probably not unlike my grandfather's felt-hat workshop, where finishing irons rested in white hot coals and vast cauldrons of stiffener and blackening bubbled and hissed hellishly. (I can remember, too, the sound of his leather bootlaces as he pulled them taut through his black Oxfords, with a high shine like a mirror on their round toes and the smell of boot polish hanging in the air around them.)

How on earth did Joe and Lou manage in such a small space with so many children? Even with the older boy, Herbert, accounted for, apprenticed to the shoemaking trade by 1883, there were still the two older girls, Julia and Martha, aged ten and seven, five-year old Beth and her two-year old sister, Evie, and a baby brother, Ernest. Anyone who has tried to entertain just one small child while attempting to work will know how much stress and strain is engendered. Who on earth could possibly stay cheerful while stopping tiny hands from constantly grabbing at hot irons or picking up sharp awls? What dirty little mites the tiniest must have been when they learned to crawl among the debris of Joe's trade.

How did Lou find the time and space to do her washing or a clean area in which to prepare food? How did she manage to keep her washing free from soot as she hung it up on wet days over the little stove in the corner of a smoky workshop? She must have wondered countless times each day whether her life would always be so difficult. Did she ever snap, threatening to walk out the door and never come back? Did she shake her babies and wish they had never been born?

-4-

"I'd done it in a minute; and, O, it cried so, Dinah –"

George Eliot, *Adam Bede*, 1859

The killing of newborn babies belongs to that half-buried, disturbing portion of human experience, the same shadowy region where incest, cannibalism and human sacrifice lurk. It is the stuff of folk tales and nightmares, a chilling primal scream that echoes down through the ages. Whenever it occurs it shatters our notions of what is natural and good and normal. And yet for a long time the practice was an accepted feature of some societies.

In the West, early Christians followed Judaic strictures regarding the sacredness of human life, but most of the European civilisations that predated the new religion had no such belief, and it's a reasonable bet that all of us who live in Europe today are descended from peoples who routinely participated in the killing of unwanted infants: baby girls, the deformed and disabled, the orphaned and the sickly.

Every schoolchild used to be taught about the Spartans, who threw their unwanted babies into the Apothetae (a ravine also known as "the place of rejection") from where there was little hope of them ever being recovered. Elsewhere in Ancient Greece, babies (especially baby girls) would be left out on hillsides, in baskets or pots, where they would either be found by someone prepared to look after them or, which was more likely, die of cold and hunger.

According to Pliny, the Ancient Romans believed that a child did not possess a soul until it was teething, and so to them the death of a young baby may not have been regarded as any more, or less, significant than is the medical abortion of "non-viable" foetuses in our own time. The Vikings followed the custom of thrusting a spear at a newborn whose birth had led to the death of its mother; if the baby grabbed the tip of the spear before it punctured its little round belly then he or she was permitted to live. The elders of early Anglo-Saxon settlements gave the father of a deformed or sickly baby the opportunity to accept it, by kneeling before the crib and taking the child in his arms; otherwise it would be put to death.

Over time in the West, the responsibility for selecting which babies were permitted to join society and which were not became less of a collective, communal matter. The elders of tribes and villages no longer instituted ceremonies and rituals to sanction the destruction of the unwanted. The practice became something that happened in secret, part of the hidden and forbidden region of human life: it was left to mothers to "do away" with those that society had no need for, and did not wish to maintain.

Beth would have grown up with tales and ballads about "changelings", children allegedly possessed by unearthly, un-Christian forces – perhaps the products of their mothers' liaisons with fairies or demon spirits. In reality, these were simply sickly, difficult children, those who were not wanted and did not belong. The changeling's usual fate was to be abandoned at a crossroads in the hope that representatives of the other world would come and take it back, perhaps leaving a mortal child in its place.

In many places, well into the nineteenth century in parts of Western Europe, it was believed that the birth of twins was "proof" of a woman's adultery. Consequently, there are many instances in folk literature of guilty women, who abandon one of their twin babies in the hope that their shame will not be discovered. In several renditions of the old, bleak ballad, *The Cruel Mother* (F. J. Child, the great Victorian collector of folk-songs, knew of at least thirteen versions current in England during the nineteenth century), the eponymous anti-heroine secretly despatches her twin, and on occasion triplet, babies in a variety of ways, including strangulation, stabbing and drowning.

As a child I had a book of ballads and would dare myself not to skip *The Cruel Mother*, with its terrifying illustration of a wild-eyed wraith, her long hair floating over the two gurgling little ones who lay within the clutches of a looming skeletal thorn. There was also a chillingly nasty playground ditty which I remember older children would whisper in the ears of younger ones (along with "informed" assurances of how you could "fall pregnant" just by sitting on a warm bus seat, or by not washing your hands after touching the door handle of a public loo). Replete with illicit thrills, the rhyme told of two lovers who meet, according to the refrain, "down the dark alley, where nobody goes". The inevitable happens: "All in blue, all in blue, she said the baby's due…", "all in red, all in red, she said the baby's dead…" Then there was the truly ghastly ballad *Weela Wallia*, which enjoyed a bit of a vogue during the folk revival of my early teens:

She stuck the knife in the baby's head,
Weela weela wallia;
The more she stabbed it the more it bled.
Down by the river Sallia

This both scared and fascinated me whenever I heard it as a young girl. It was usually sung in such a jocular fashion – was it meant to be funny? If so, what tough lessons still existed between me and the adult world? I knew so much and yet, I reasoned, my heart sinking at the prospect, there was still so much else to learn. The reed banks of the River Sallia, the filthy dark alley and the bleak thorn-strewn greenwood-side were the places of nightmare where I would return again and again: the sites of an atavistic compulsion to shed my innocence in the inevitable surrender to darkness and maturity.

Encountering the anti-heroines of these scraps of folk-memory, along with more literary incarnations of the "cruel" mother (Effie Deans in Walter Scott's *The Heart of Midlothian*, or Hetty Sorrell in George Eliot's *Adam Bede*, for example), and the real murdering mothers, like Beth, when they crop up in the court reports and the minutes of lunacy commissions or as footnotes to psychiatric research papers, is hardly a comforting matter. They are rarely presented as anything more then ciphers; they are for the most part inarticulate and amnesiac (indeed, mothers who commit infanticide rarely purport to remember anything of the act itself, perhaps suffering from some form of post-traumatic amnesia), blank spaces on to which the details have been sketched in by others, if at all. They are deplorable sinners, pathetic victims of man's lust, hormonally defined and driven, inhuman monsters, women who love too much, helpless vessels of nature's whims and mysteries. They are subject to the indifference, the fear, the pity and the loathing of society at large, and drawn and redrawn in its image.

And if the women are no more than ghostly smudges on the pages of history and medical textbooks, then their babies are even more absent from the telling. The legends and songs reflect a harsh reality which had nothing to do with fairies and enchantments. We can imagine all too easily the real fate of all those babies abandoned at forsaken spots on the edges of towns and villages, or in deep, dark forests where wild animals prowled. Those little ghosts, hovering above the world they hardly knew, are invariably denied any individual identity; they are often of indeterminate sex, the inevitable casualties of Malthusian equanimity or biochemical imbalance. They appear in the records as charred bundles of bones buried in suburban gardens, or stuffed into tree hollows. They are discovered mummified beneath the floorboards of nondescript rooms, bloated cherubs fished from dirty canals, strangled with ribbons or bootlaces, stabbed with pins, decapitated with razors, put out with the rubbish in bin-liners or supermarket carrier bags, drowned in railway station and airport toilets: dumped, concealed, smothered, unwanted.

In early modern Britain, unwanted children were primarily the illegitimate; that is, those children whose fathers were not prepared, or were unable, to recognise and support them. These babies were a constant reminder of their mother's shame; to the community at large, they were the tangible proof of the existence of sin. Many of them were disposed of almost as soon as they drew breath. In all the available official statistics of infant homicide and mortality from the past, illegitimate babies are disproportionately represented. The 1624 Act to Prevent the Destroying and Murthering of Bastard Children specifically targeted "lewd", unmarried women who, it was alleged, were in the habit of secretly burying or otherwise concealing the death of their infant children, in order "to avoid their shame, and to escape punishment..." At the time of the Act, unless she could find a man who was prepared to support her and her offspring, a single mother faced a miserable round of punishment and interrogation (even midwives were instructed to question women during labour, in order that the baby's father could be identified and ordered to support the child).

Everything was done to try and deter the single mother from claiming the meagre parish relief that was her entitlement. A year in the local House of Correction, followed by many more of penury and shame on the fringes of society, cannot have been a very inviting prospect for those women who fell pregnant outside marriage. It is therefore perhaps not surprising that so many of them appear to have opted for "concealment", denying, perhaps even to themselves, that they were ever pregnant, and doing away with their babies moments after having given birth, most likely alone under a hayrick or in a ditch. Where women were able to give birth in a room of their own, in the house of a parent or employer, they, as was frequently reported, muffled their own labouring cries with rags, which they then stuffed into the maw of their newborn infant son or daughter.

Where the offence was found out (and in close-knit communities, and the overcrowded living conditions of the past, it was almost inevitable that their pregnancy would be noticed by somebody) these women usually claimed in desperation that their baby had been born dead or had been accidentally smothered when the mother had attempted to give the child suck. Deaths by overlaying are a regular feature of the Bills of Mortality. Some of the deaths recorded as such may well have been accidental (it was not until 1971 that Sudden Infant Death Syndrome – SIDS – was officially recognised as a certifiable cause of death by the Registrar General and the Coroners' Society of England and Wales). After all, many poverty-stricken mothers drank heavily in order to forget the misery of their existence, or went to their beds exhausted after a hard day's labouring in fields and factories. But it is also true that many desperate women deliberately smothered their babies in the days following childbirth; in fact there are many instances of women convicted of "making away" with not just one but several of their unfortunate offspring, almost as if infanticide were a substitute for other methods of family planning.

After 1624, the penalty for infanticide was very severe: "death, as in the case of murther, except such mother can make proof by one witness at the last that the child was born dead". The Act resulted in the hanging of many mothers over the next hundred and eighty years, yet, even so, there is no evidence that the harsh penalty acted as much of a deterrent. With few plausible alternatives available to them, women continued to murder their unwanted babies all through the seventeenth and eighteenth centuries. The 1624 Act was eventually repealed in 1803 (although women continued to be hanged for the murder of their babies for several decades after that, and they continued to be tried for murder until 1922, when infanticide became a separate category of homicide in English law, facing the same class of penalty as the lesser charge of manslaughter), and for the rest of the nineteenth century in Britain babies made up more than sixty per cent of homicide victims (even though they only formed three per cent of the total population). There are some estimates that the incidence of infant homicide in the nineteenth century was probably at least ten times higher than the official records.

The staggeringly high infant mortality rates of the time are usually attributed to the terrible poverty endured by the majority of families, especially those forced into the city slums. Certainly, a great many babies died from neglect, usually as the result of abandonment. Others died because their parents were so poor and so ill-educated that they were unable to satisfy even the most basic sanitary and dietary requirements of a small child. This was the particular fate of babies born to those who had recently moved in search of work to the towns and cities of Victorian England, where germs were far more pervasive than in the country, and where women found themselves distanced from the networks of support and knowledge which had hitherto sustained generations of new mothers.

A great many babies died, too, when they were left in the care of others, by mothers forced to travel far away in search of work or seeking to conceal the existence of illegitimate offspring. Before regulatory measures were put in place in 1872, up to ninety per cent of babies left in the care of the notorious Victorian baby-farms died.

Babies were more vulnerable than anyone else, and they were more at risk of dying a violent death than any other group. Indeed, before compulsory registration of births became law in England in 1874, it was surprisingly easy to do away with a baby. (Stillbirths remained outside the scope of the registration legislation until the 1920s.) Coroners, where they were involved at all, tended to return a murder verdict only in a very few, clear-cut cases of sudden infant death. They were loath to condemn the impoverished, exhausted, lactating, recently delivered women who frequently appeared before them and were content to give them the benefit of the doubt. One nine-teenth-century Home Secretary described such cases as "the most distressing... that come before one..."

But, then as now, it was not just poor, desperate single mothers who killed their babies. Although most serious considerations of the history of infanticide tend to concentrate on these cases, cases involving so-called "respectable married women", with no record of cruelty or neglect towards their other children, women such as my great-grandmother, were not at all rare in the past. Research by Dr Jonathan Andrews of Oxford Brookes University has shown that seventy-four per cent of women admitted to Broadmoor for infanticide between 1863-1914 were married women, generally, like Beth, drawn from the lower reaches of the middling class. There is other research which supports this finding, and suggests that throughout the nineteenth century most cases of puerperal psychosis admitted to mental institutions were married multigravids.

It was the respectable, married baby-killers who really perplexed Victorian society (and still disturb us today), throwing the moral suppositions upon which so much of our judicial system is predicated into chaos. In the past, in such cases, there was simply no other explanation: these women had to be mad and therefore they were more likely to be admitted to lunatic asylums than were their unmarried sisters.

Is there a mother on earth who has not at some point found herself in the middle of the night threatening her tiny child with a violent death? Obviously most of us have not thrown our babies out the window, or, Lady Macbeth-like, dashed their brains against the nearest wall, but that realisation should possibly make us more understanding of the mothers who did, and who are not now in a position to laugh at the memory of such desperation, and never will be.

In a letter to the *British Medical Journal*, published shortly before his death in 2002, John Emery, Professor Emeritus of Paediatric Pathology at the University of Sheffield (and the expert credited with first drawing attention to SIDS in a seminal paper published in 1956), asserted that in "hundreds of confidential inquiries into sudden, unexpected deaths [of infants], the most usual scenario for filicide is for the baby to have been suffocated by an exhausted parent (usually the mother) while trying to quieten his or her crying." Emery, whose pioneering work in the field spanned more than forty years, went on to emphasise his belief that "these parents usually barely know what they were doing and did not intend or want to kill their child." This observation must hold true in respect of the past, as much as it ought to do today. Emery concludes in his letter, "We need to prevent these deaths, not victimise the parents." If the death of their child is the very worst thing most mothers can imagine, how much worse it must be to live with the knowledge that your child died as a direct result of something you, its mother, did or did not do. Most mothers are quick to blame themselves for every bad thing that happens to their children – guilt comes with the territory – but what must it be like to live with that level of guilt? To grieve for a dead child and to wake every morning to profound feelings of loss, desolation, and the awful knowledge that you killed your own baby.

The archetype of self-sacrificial, unconditional, instinctual maternal love is a standard to which we all aspire. We want to believe that mothers are good, that the love between a mother and her baby is inviolable and eternal. (What I found difficult whenever I thought about Beth was reconciling my inchoate perception of her as a cruel witch, capable of drowning her babies like so many kittens, with the cosy image of a benign pastry-cook and prodigious needlewoman, a wife, mother and grandmother who loved and was loved. How can someone be both I asked myself?) And we are just as perplexed now as ever that gentle, passive, loving people can wreak destruction and chaos: caring mothers, we reason, do not drown their babies in cold rainwater.

Oh, but they do.

-5-
"Needlepin, needlepin, stitch upon stitch"

Lou was, as her own mother had been, a working mother. They both held fast to the old idea that a shilling you earn yourself is worth two given you by a man. And they would have been nonplussed by the degree to which modern working mothers beat themselves up as we try to juggle the conflicting demands of work and family. Guilt, in this respect, was a feeling which only crept into the hearts of the women in my family as they began to venture up the ladder towards the rung of middle class (Beth's generation). Before then, for a very long time, it was self-evident that everyone in a family – men, women, children, old and young alike – did whatever it took to avoid being out at their heels.

Once she was married, Lou, like most shoemakers' wives, helped her husband with the finishing; that is, by stitching together the uppers of the shoes he made. But she had been a wage-earner long before she was married. From the age of six, until her death just before her sixtieth birthday, Lou worked at the lace. All her close female relatives were lace-makers, as were most of her female friends and neighbours. Lou would not have thought twice about encouraging her daughters into the trade, even though it was actually in decline by the time they were born and would be altogether finished by the turn of the twentieth century. As far as Lou was concerned lace-making was a useful skill, and a woman who has a useful skill will always be ahead of the game. By passing on her skills to her daughters she was teaching them to be independent and self-sufficient, just as girls of later generations were encouraged to learn typing and shorthand so we would always have "something to fall back on".

Lou's second daughter, Martha, spent most of her childhood with her mother's parents, living with them on and off for more than ten years until their deaths when she was in her late teens; for most of that time, until she was offered an alternative, she plied the lace trade alongside her granny, helping to support herself and the elderly couple. It had been illegal since 1864 to give employment to the under-eights, and the 1860s and 1870s saw numerous progressive laws come into force which sought to regulate the hours and conditions of employment for under-thirteens. But these laws were designed to combat abuses in factories and workshops, whereas lace was worked at home, with grandmothers, mothers and aunties supervising. It was consequently very difficult to police the conditions under which hundreds of little girls were employed. What is more, the pennies brought in by these little girls kept many indigent families "off the parish", and the situation was generally tolerated as the lesser of two evils.

The Education Act of 1876 had, in effect, made school attendance compulsory for all those aged less than ten years, and Beth was therefore one of the first in her family to go to school on a regular basis. Parents were compelled to pay a few hard-to-come-by pennies each day, and School Attendance Officers were employed by local school boards (in Potterspury it was John Reid and his son Walter who were the scourge of Beth and her siblings) to ensure that the children of the poor learnt to read and write. But school only occupied, at most, the hours between 9.30am. and 4.30pm. There was no means of controlling what children did in the hours before and after the school day, or at weekends and during the holidays. And there was very little that schools could do if parents kept children off on occasion to help them at home or at work. It was against the law to permit a child of thirteen years of age or less to work between the hours of 7pm and 6am. But who knew what went on behind cottage doors in the hours of darkness, and who was going to report their neighbours to the authorities for incursions of which they were themselves every bit as guilty?

So it was that anyone taking a turn about the Potterspury of Beth's childhood on a fine day would have seen (as Shakespeare has Orsino observe) maids in every cottage doorway weaving their threads with bone. In summer when the nights were short, women and girls would sit at their doorways until late, throwing conversation, songs and rhymes across the street to one another. Wandering through the villages in that corner of north Buckinghamshire/Northamptonshire it would have been hard to keep count of the numbers of girls and women of all ages, in their crisp white aprons, stooped over their wooden "horses". These were tall three-legged stools, topped with bulbous Hessian pillows. The pillows were stuffed with straw, covered with bright calico prints, and stuck with pins arranged in intricate patterns, from which spangly bobbins dangled and creamy bands of fine Bucks point lacework flowed.

When I was a child my grandfather had a little wooden box full of lace bobbins, and when we were bored my sister and I would take them out and play with them. Some of the bobbins were made of bone and had names and phrases pricked out on their skinny shafts, which you could only read by turning them carefully between your thumb and forefinger. Among the names I remember were those of Beth's mother and grandmother and their husbands, illuminated in little coloured dots of black, green and red, and decorated with tiny hearts. My grandfather was, as ever, obdurate in his refusal to explain the origins of the bobbins. I do not even recall him telling me that they had come to him from his mother. But he must have done for when years later I discovered his grandmother and great-grandmother on the census, listed as lace-makers, I remembered that I had always known that.

Tantalisingly, there were some bobbins that still had a wisp of fine cotton thread wrapped around them, as if the owner had simply left off in the middle of her work one day and never returned to it again. I thought they were lovely things, with their delicately carved spindles and clusters of pretty coloured glass beads at the end. I had no idea then of the lives of relentless toil with which they were associated. It was the evident pride, the desire to make mundane things as cheerful and pleasant as possible which was impressed upon me.

***

Today, when we visit tranquil and picturesque villages, it is hard to imagine the populous and lively places they must once have been. Gangs of raggedy, grimy kids whooping and scuffling as they chase each other down the lanes; the clatter of pots and gossip clamouring from the backs of tenements, each sound ringing through the open air; the robust smells from numerous pigsties mingling with those from the middens and outhouses; billows of sooty smoke pouring from crooked chimneys. On wet days and in the evenings the local inns would be full of the village men, talking and drinking as the steam rose off their damp, rough tweeds, blending with the smoke from the clay pipes which they all clenched in the corner of their mouths, into one great cloud of acrid eye-stinging fug. Only when night fell would a village become as peaceful and still as they are nowadays, with just the trees creaking down the chimneys and the wind grumbling as it turned the corners. Then the lights in the cottage windows would go out one by one until only one or two winked faintly through the tracery of the elm boughs. Silence would settle, only occasionally pierced by the whirr of a nighthawk, or a fox splashing through the mud of the ditches and barking for his mate.

Most people, certainly most men, who started work at dawn, went to their beds soon after sundown – after all, it was expensive to light candles and keep the fire going. But the low and the desperate (which everyone became from time to time) had no choice but to keep going with their work. When, in pinch times, Lou and her mother and sisters carried on with their lace-making past nightfall, they would cover the cottage windows with pieces of rag so that nobody would know that they needed to work, their only light coming from a candle stub set into a glass flask filled with iced water to intensify the glow. The light fell in brilliant near-perfect spots on their pillows.

On chilly nights, when the man and the babes were still about, they would have to keep the door ajar to let out the smoke from the fire and protect the lace from the smuts and soot. But when they were on their own the fire would be extinguished and they would keep themselves warm by filling brass or earthenware fire-pots with hot ashes from the grate, placing them under their feet and tucking their skirts around to keep the heat in. They were cosy enough as they sat breathing in the fumes, trying to ignore the sting of their chilblains. As the evening drew on they sat in a tight circle, murmuring soft conversation to one another so as not to waken the man or the little-uns, their heads bent over the work as they nimbly threaded the wisps of fine cotton in and out of the little maze of pins before them, the spangles hanging from their bobbins chinking each time they were disturbed.

Lou and her mother, and most of the women they knew, had been put to work in lace schools from five years of age, when they were still nimble enough to develop the required dexterity and impressionable enough to develop the necessary patience and the low expectations that went with the job. The so-called "lace schools" were in reality no more than a cottage room where several girls would sit in silence for six or seven hours at a time, learning the craft in exchange for a sixpence. In addition, lace schools served the useful purpose of providing childcare for working mothers. Beth and her sisters may have attended a lace school in Potterspury (there was one still operating in the village in the early part of the twentieth century), but it is more likely that they were taught at home by their mother and grandmother, as they enlisted the girls to help them complete their orders.

Some lace schools used rough methods to inculcate the children in their care: it was not uncommon for little girls to have their noses or hands rubbed raw against the rows of pins for the "crime" of "looking off the pillow". Other schools taught the girls in their charge to read and write, as well as make lace, but Beth's grandmother never learnt how to write her own name, and it was only after her marriage to Joe, a literate shoemaker, that Lou did so.

Lace-making women kept their hands very clean and wore spotless starched aprons over their clothes (all in order to protect the lace). But lace-makers were not known for their domesticity or for the "quality time" they expended on their offspring. The hours they worked were very long, as much as ten to twelve hours a day, and so there was little time left over for ordinary household chores and all but the most basic childcare. Their babies were frequently dosed with a tot of Godfrey's Cordial, and the older children left to fend for themselves.

The conditions under which these women laboured, working in close proximity to one another, in overcrowded and ill-ventilated cottages, were breeding grounds for disease. In 1831 and 1849 two major cholera epidemics spread rapidly among lace workers in north Buckinghamshire. Young female lace workers were twice as likely to die of tuberculosis and lung disease than were the young men in their families; they also suffered with bad eyesight, chilblains, oedema, recurring headaches and a whole host of digestive problems, all as a result of spending long hours of each day stooped over the pillows, peering at the intricate patterns before them. And although the money they earned (perhaps not much more than a penny an hour) often equalled the wages of their husbands, and was the only factor keeping many a labourer's family out of the workhouse, their efforts were rarely appreciated by those outside the home. They were routinely accused of being "slatternly" and "neglectful", of keeping filthy cottages and of being little better than prostitutes, a trade to which, it was often claimed, they resorted from time to time.

The lace-maker's world was a very feminine one, with hours of each day spent in the company of female relatives and neighbours. They had the confidence women have when they spend all day together, swapping experiences and remedies, gossiping about one another and their men, children, elderly parents and neighbours, graphically describing their health concerns, helping each other out with childcare, food and clothing. They also had the self-assurance that comes with earning more than the sullen dullards in clodhopper boots that made up the male population of their villages. Until they married one of their own, that is, and before the years of stooping at the pillow interspersed with bouts of childbearing formed humps on their young, straight backs, wrinkled the smooth, fair skin around their bright eyes, distended their firm bellies: before all of that befell them, lace-makers could afford to cut a dash with nice clothes and bouncing curls.

Respectability is largely a subjective matter. Their work might have been hard, but lace makers considered them-selves to be far better, in every way, than the poor gleaners, the wives of agricultural labourers who had no such skilled calling, and who scrabbled over the stubble after harvest, clutching in the pocket of their backs handfuls of grain-pecks which the rake had missed. Lace-makers would have shuddered with distaste when observing the rough gangers walking home from the fields, with their torn dresses and unkempt locks, their bones gnarled by the damp. Lace girls could take their pick of any man in the village because they were whip smart and had independent means. Female gangers, by contrast, were drunkards, had casual sex in haystacks and gave birth in ditches. And my lace-making ancestresses would definitely have counted themselves better off than some poor skivvy, slaving away in a big house, far away from her mum and sisters and girlfriends, and entirely at the mercy of petulant chatelaines, bad-tempered cooks, and predatory masters and male servants.

And yet "gregarious employment", runs a common Victorian observation, "gives a slang appearance to girls", and no matter how good they thought they were, the lace girls found it was impossible to avoid the unwarranted disapproval of others, and a reputation for "commonness". It was disgraceful, said the many middle-class observers, bemoaning the chronic servant shortage in the lace-making districts, the way these girls preferred to earn their keep by sitting in cottage doorways chatting to one another and flirting with passing ploughboys. Why, it appeared that they actually preferred this scabrous life-style to a more honest one spent down on their knees scrubbing someone else's flagstones! How thoroughly opprobrious it was that these flashy girls preferred to dangle a lace pillow and bobbins on their knees, than the babies of their betters. Lace-makers were condemned for taking frivolous pains over their personal appearance, for keeping their hands as clean and white as a lady's and for trimming their cheap calico frocks and straw bonnets with odd scraps of fancy lace edging. But, most damning of all, they were accused of being bad mothers.

There were many complaints about the sons of lace-makers who, left to fend for themselves, roamed village streets in gangs causing trouble with their rowdy games of "clink and bandy", chucking stones at bottles and cats, making swings by tying together willow boughs, and illegally fishing with bent pins and lengths of thread. The lace-makers' daughters, girls such as Beth and her sisters, were less of a problem. There was plenty to keep them occupied: minding baby brothers and sisters, fetching the tea for their fathers, helping their mothers keep up with the washing and mending and, of course, learning the lace. There was not a great deal of pleasure in their young lives.

***

Perhaps as many as a fifth of all children born to the poor in the nineteenth century would not have survived much past their first year. Infant mortality was not as high in country hovels as it was in urban slums, but it was still high enough to account for a hundred out of every thousand born throughout Victoria's reign. It would be reasonable therefore to expect that Lou might have lost at least one of her children in the first four years or so after birth; yet there is no evidence that she did.

Like her mother before her, Lou seems to have managed her family very well indeed. She does not appear to have had any children at all for the first two years of her married life (unless she lost one or more through stillbirth or miscarriage, which would not have appeared on the register), and thereafter she gave birth to a total of six children at three to four year intervals. And it is a fact that all Lou's brood went on to lead relatively long lives.

It certainly is a mystery how she managed this impressive achievement, when she spent all her married life in cramped, poorly-ventilated rooms with no proper sanitation, always struggling to make ends meet. She achieved it in part, no doubt, by working all the hours she could to bring in extra cash, and by going without food herself, when necessary, to ensure that Joe and the children had their share.

It may well be that the strenuous lives the lace-makers led, working long hours of every day yet never rising much above base poverty, subsisting on meagre diets lacking in many basic nutrients, induced bouts of amenorrhoea during which they were unable to conceive. Or that the rigours of their lives left the women, and their men, too exhausted to have sex more than very occasionally. However, Lou and Joe clearly sustained a sexual interest in one another for at least twenty years, as their last child was born when they were in their early forties (a common occurrence in the past, when women wrongly assumed that they were "through the change", only to "get caught out").

Abstinence was frequently advocated in the nineteenth and early twentieth centuries by their social betters as an approved method by which the poor could limit the burdens which their large families placed upon them (and the rest of society). Although, it was also cautioned, this was a solution only to be used by those staunch few whose nerves were up to the challenge. I am sure that my ancestors were just as mindful as anyone of their responsibilities to the children they already had. Perhaps they resorted to the old tried and tested method of, as one Victorian woman expressed it, "pushing him out of the way when I think it's near..." – although, as with abstinence, there were also concerns that the withdrawal method could be "hurtful to the nervous system in many persons".

Contrary to the popular idea of "sexless" Victorian ancestors, who nonetheless somehow produced enormous families, there is plenty of evidence that from the 1850s onwards couples were actively controlling the numbers of children they had. During the period Lou and Joe were producing their children, there was a sharp decline in the English birth-rate, particularly marked after 1876. The term "birth control" did not come into use until World War One, but "preventatives" and "checks" certainly existed in the nineteenth century; in fact this was a period of many advances in contraception. The methods available to ordinary people were divided into the "artificial" and the "natural", or "Malthusian" (in honour of the economist, Thomas Robert Malthus, whose arguments for population control, by famine, disease and war, formed the basis for many of the social reforms in the 1830s and 1840s). In 1876 Annie Besant, later a leading light of the Fabian movement, and the campaigning journalist and MP Charles Bradlaugh disseminated an American pamphlet, *The Fruits of Philosophy* – generally regarded as the first advocacy of modern birth control. Society was not ready, however, and the pair found themselves in court on immorality and obscenity charges (and Besant later lost custody of her child as a result of her continued promotion of contraception – a topic the London *Times* described as "indecent, lewd, filthy, bawdy and obscene").

Dr. H. Arthur Allbutt's *The Wife's Handbook* was first published in 1886, and carried a chapter on "preventatives" as well as advertisements for various products. Allbutt also directed women to inspect their vaginas with a small mirror so that they would learn how to recognise the changes indicative of pregnancy, "or better still" ask their husbands or female friends and neighbours to have a look for them. The General Medical Council struck Allbutt off the Medical Register in 1888 for his well-intentioned contribution "to the detriment of public morals", but he had the last laugh. His book (which cost an affordable 6d) was a bestseller. It ran into thirty-five editions in just twelve years, and was still in print and widely read in the 1920s. There is every possibility that my grandfather would have had a copy, and so too might his parents and grandparents.

Sheaths or "letters", generally made of skin or thin India rubber, had been available for a very long time. In the 1870s and 1880s they cost between 3/- and 10/- a dozen (the thinner the rubber the more expensive). Originally devised as a means of preventing the spread of venereal disease, they retained in some sections of the population their unsavoury association with prostitution, and many people felt they served no other purpose than the promotion of immorality. There were other methods available, designed for woman to use: celluloid Dutch caps, which had the advantage that they "lasted a lifetime" and "circular rubber sheaths" which could be purchased for between 3/- and 5/- a dozen.

There was also a whole range of spermicidal "contraceptive powders" and "solutions" (usually containing quinine and boric acid) which were to be inserted into the vagina "before connection", via syringe, douche, sponge, or a contraption called the "insufflator" – a rubber bulb attached to a length of tubing which could be employed to blow the powder into the vagina. The powders and solutions could be purchased for about 5/- a dozen, if you knew where from and had the readies.

In the 1880s the "Wife's Friend", a pessary (quinine solution again, this time in a soluble cocoa-butter coating) came on to the market. At 2/- per dozen these were cheaper than many of the alternatives and became very popular among the aspirant upper working classes.

It is impossible to determine how many women, especially those outside the middle classes, were able, and indeed so inclined, to take advantage of these advances. It is however easy to imagine what their reasons for not doing so might have been. In the first place, it was pro-bably very difficult for women like Lou, living in rural areas, to obtain information about contraceptive devices, let alone the goods themselves. Doctors were generally against them, and not just on moral grounds. It was difficult to ensure the scrupulous personal hygiene required when inserting sponges, tubes and syringes into the vagina if you lived in an overcrowded hovel with no running water. Many of these products were intrinsically unhygienic, and the utilisation of them could lead to dangerous infections of the reproductive system and urinary tract. Many doctors also suspected, and not without reason, that the powders themselves contributed to the incidence of uterine, and other cancers.

Setting aside the objections raised by the medical profession, there is a certain amount of anecdotal evidence that many working-class women were themselves resistant to the idea of "using precautions". They believed it was actually sinful to use artificial preventatives, and grappled with their conscience before doing so. Those who lived in small villages would have found it nigh-on impossible to obtain such products without risking hurtful gossip and even ostracism. "What did you get married for if you don't want to have children?" was an objection often flung in the face of women who complained about their lot. Even if they were able to tough out the condemnation of their more narrow-minded neighbours, many couples would have found the devices beyond the reach of their meagre income in any case. Lou and Joe, for example, would rarely have earned more than £1 a week (not much more than the equivalent of £52 nowadays), barely enough to cover their rent, and clothe and feed themselves and their children. They would have been mindful of spending money they could ill afford, especially on items which might not even work. The advertisements for contraceptive devices might have claimed that they were "thoroughly reliable", but in practice there was no guarantee. Modern spermicidal preparations only guarantee seventy five per cent effectiveness against pregnancy, and we can safely presume that their Victorian equivalents would have been far less successful.

Perhaps Lou and her peers had other, tried and trusted methods of family planning at their disposal. The eminent birth-control historian, Angus McLaren, suggests that abortion had been "both a supplement and an alternative to contraception" for the majority of women for a very long time. Contemporary nineteenth-century estimates reckoned that as many as a quarter of all pregnancies ended in an untimely way at the contrivance of the mother. (This is more or less in line with the proportion of conceptions that end in abortion today in England and Wales: 175,600 in 2002, representing about twenty three per cent of all conceptions). It is more than likely that most poor women, up until the middle of the last century would have resorted to abortion at least once in their lifetime (as did a high percentage of middle class women).

This comparatively drastic, frequently dangerous, method of family planning prevailed in the face of egregious objection. The medical profession took a very dim view of the "terrible crime of abortion", not just on moral grounds but largely because the practice led to the deaths of so many women. Abortion had been illegal in English law since 1803, and the Offences Against the Person Act, 1861, made it illegal to procure a miscarriage; and anyone found guilty of supplying or using a "poison or other noxious instrument" to induce abortion faced life imprisonment. A great deal of publicity was given to those occasions when a desperate woman, having paid £3 to a midwife or a quack doctor, died from the gangrenous effects of a lacerated and punctured uterus.

Most poor women, however, saw to such things themselves as soon as they noticed any "irregularity" in their cycle. They would drink an infusion of dried tansy leaves and hot water last thing at night, and the next morning they would, hopefully, have their period again. Or they would take some pennyroyal in tea with a tablespoon of Brewer's Yeast added to it to make it more effective. It was a commonly held belief that as long as the "necessary" was carried out before the third month, that is before the quickening of the foetus was felt, it was "all right". After that only a very bad woman would attempt such a thing for fear of what harm it would do to her baby. This belief probably forms the sad reasoning behind the prejudice and horror with which birth defects were popularly regarded from early times until well into the twentieth century. In the past women carried the guilt and blame for everything, even those areas of life over which they had no control or understanding. No doubt the accepted wisdom of attempting self-abortion by the third month had been learnt through custom, trial and error, for there is a sound medical reasoning behind it. Any abortifacient should be taken as soon as possible after the first missed monthly period; that is, by the sixth week after conception, and certainly by the eighth week, when the risk of incomplete abortion is greatest. By that time the foetus will be about an inch long and too large to pass through the cervix on its own. A woman attempting to self-abort at that time will probably haemorrhage, and anything that remains inside her will almost certainly putrefy, giving rise to a potentially fatal infection. Nowadays an incomplete abortion, or miscarriage, will be remedied by a D and C, but not in the past.

Either way, for the most part it was simply a common-sensical belief among the great mass of ordinary women, that it was less "sinful" to induce a miscarriage in the early phase of pregnancy than it was to purchase and use "dirty" and "shameful" contraceptive devices. My grandmother (who was comparatively enlightened about such matters) often recalled her time helping out in a chemist shop in Pontypridd during World War Two. She thought it quite amusing when local women ("even quite respectable ones", as she put it) visited the shop with convoluted explanations as to why they wanted to purchase lengths of slippery elm bark or oil of pennyroyal. Chemists were forbidden by law, of course, from providing anything which they suspected might be used to bring about an abortion, so desperate women would often resort to sending their mothers, husbands, and even their children, to acquire the items in their place.

Many of the remedies women passed on to each other probably did nothing worse than induce a bout of vomiting, but some were positively dangerous. Rue, for example, an ancient emmenagogue which features prominently in folklore (and in Ophelia's "mad speech" in *Hamlet*, where its double meaning of bitterness and regret is used to poetic effect), is highly toxic if too much is taken in a single dose. In the past, women must have known precisely how much to take over a given period of time in order to avoid poisoning themselves.

Tansy, which used to grow in plentiful supply in the hedgerows of England and was used in cooking by many poor country families (such as the one Beth grew up in), would have endangered the health of any woman using it over the long term, especially if she had a kidney complaint or blood-clotting disorder or suffered from epilepsy. And it was not just the herbal home remedies which were dangerous. A number of shop-bought preparations included the substance diachylon, for example, which is high in lead. Yet millions of women, our ancestors, persisted in the practice of self-aborting, or "bringing on their monthlies", as older women in my family euphemistically called it, well into the last century.

In addition to taking toxins, they threw themselves downstairs, jumped off the copper, vigorously beat all their rugs and carpets, went for long walks or a ride in a jolting dicky cart, swallowed pins and inserted knitting needles, tightened their girdles and corsets, did strenuous exercises with rolling-pins, and drank gin, hot water, castor oil, Epsom salts, or other concoctions made with parsley (a mild emmenagogue which was a popular recommendation in the girls' lavatories of my own teens). I am sure that Lou was familiar with at least a couple of these solutions and had one or two of her own as well. And if they failed to work, and you were caught out, then you simply had to carry on as best you could with your latest little "blessing".

***

As Beth grew up it became harder and harder not only for Joe to sell his boots, but also for Lou to sell her lace whenever the family income needed a boost. Joe would travel hopefully to market with his samples only to come home cursing those who were no better than he was, but who had, by some twist of fate, acquired mastery over him. Lou and Martha were continuing to take the lace made by them and the girls of the family to the dealers, but by the 1880s the pinch was on. The local haberdashers the women sold to were also the people from whom they bought the parchment patterns, the threads and the pins which were their raw materials. An unscrupulous dealer might urge on Lou materials which she neither wanted nor needed, and then take anyway for the items from the money paid out for the finished lace. Lace-makers tried to free themselves from the dealers. Many were prepared to walk long distances to deliver lace made to private order, but here again they were entirely at the mercy of the deceitfulness, cupidity and whims of their customers. No doubt Beth accompanied her mother on many ten- or fifteen-mile hikes to the homes of grand ladies, only to be told by a contumelious housekeeper that fashions had changed and the mistress no longer wanted the lace.

As Beth reached her teens the rejections and the humiliations her mother faced would have been routine. From the 1890s onwards, the increased production of machine-lace effectively killed off the hand-worked cottage trade, so long a mainstay of Lou's, just as the shoe factories killed off the craftsmanship of men like Joe. Non-profit-making philanthropic organisations, such as the North Bucks Lace Association, were established to meet the challenges posed by such bewildering change. The organisations tried to help those who kept at the trade as their mothers and grandmothers had before them, assuming they would always be able to rely on it to help them through, and not really knowing what else they could turn their hand to. But the fact remained that nobody wanted the delicate strips of simple honeycomb picked out with creamy gimp, when they could have yards of the factory stuff with its fancy birds and blousy roses for the same money.

Beth must have grown accustomed to her parents' anxiety, as the world which they had known so well receded and everything that replaced it was harder to succeed at. I guess that this was the point at which she acquired her lifelong dread of ruin. How many times they must have wondered how they would live without resorting to the shameful practice of going cap in hand to the guardians at the workhouse, asking for out-relief. Every day her dad and visitors to the shop would have made that common observation of the Victorian rural poor, "They live better in the workhouse than we do here", rounded with a bitter laugh. Of course there was no way that Joe would ever find his way to the workhouse gate. He would rather have starved in the gutter than willingly relinquish his dignity and pride. The shame of coming to such an end was almost as great as that attached to prison or the gallows, or the insane asylum.

In Potterspury in the early twentieth century a farmer's wife started to buy the bulk of the lace still being produced by the village women (as did several vicars' wives elsewhere in Buckinghamshire and Northamptonshire) in a well-intentioned attempt to preserve the cottage industry and the independence it gave to poor women. Classes were set up for child lace-makers in an attempt to give them much-needed employment and to maintain the standard and quality of the end product, so much more beautiful than the factory stuff. But it was all too late, for by then the lace trade really was finished and the few lace-makers who were left were reduced to posing for picture postcards depicting their quaint custom and appearance. As far as Beth was concerned, lace would eventually become something with which she decorated her windows and trimmed her cushion covers, and which she placed, stitched into neat little circles, under her knick-knacks.

-6-
"Down the dark alley…"

In Devizes, on 23rd August 1849, Rebecca Smith, the wife of a violent drunkard, was publicly hanged, having been convicted of poisoning seven of her newborn babies. She did so, she claimed, out of a fear that otherwise they would "come to want". According to a contemporary broadsheet, she "acknowledged the justice of the punishment that awaited her and frequently expressed a hope that others would take a warning by her fate". Smith was the last woman to be hanged in Britain for the murder of her infant child. In fact, since the mid-nineteenth century, women who have confessed to killing their babies have in general been treated much more leniently than those found guilty of other categories of homicide, and much more leniently than fathers who have killed their babies.

The 1922 Infanticide Act created a separate felony, infanticide, defined as the killing of a newly born child by its mother not fully recovered from the effects of giving birth. It carried a maximum sentence of life imprisonment, although most of the women convicted of infanticide since 1922 have not received a custodial sentence. Previously, women accused of killing their babies were tried for murder, and many of those found guilty stood in the dock while the judge donned his black cap and intoned the dread words, "that you be taken from hence to the place from where you came, and from there to a place of execution…" Although in practice judges nearly always recommended the commutation of the death sentence, the unfortunate creature in the dock often had no reason to believe that she would escape the gallows. Between 1849 and 1900, thirty women found guilty of the murder of their babies were eventually reprieved only after what must have been a terrifying stay in the condemned cell.

Mothers who killed their *older* babies and children, however, often did hang, especially where the circumstances of the murder offended moral sensibility. The first British person to hang in the twentieth century was Louise Massett, on January 9th 1900, who battered to death her three-year-old illegitimate son, Manfred, in order that she could elope with a lover. Massett was not only of questionable virtue, she was also, crucially, unable to make any excuses for herself on the grounds of diminished responsibility. But such instances notwithstanding, for much of the nineteenth and early twentieth centuries British judges were loath to pass the mandatory death sentence on women who killed their children, or even to commit them to a term in prison. Such women were much more likely to be placed in a mental institution.

This legislative tendency to leniency continues today in Britain, and in the thirty other countries that have infanticide statutes. Mothers who kill their babies are still far more likely to find themselves the subject of a probationary order and placed in the care of psychiatric services than to face a custodial sentence. This is largely because, since 1849, the mental health of a newly delivered mother convicted of infanticide has usually been taken into account: a principal enshrined in English law. Section 1 of the Infanticide Act of 1938 (still in force) states that a woman who has wilfully, or by omission, caused the death of her child under the age of twelve months will be punished as if she were guilty of manslaughter rather than murder, if it can be found that "at the time of the act or omission the balance of her mind was disturbed by reason of her not having fully recovered from the effect of giving birth to the child or by reason of the effect of lactation consequent upon the birth of the child..."

The idea of a newly delivered mother's diminished responsibility had been in currency for some time. Back in 1783 the renowned "man-midwife", Dr. William Hunter, had argued that whereas every female creature possessed a natural maternal passion, a woman who had just gone through the ordeal of childbirth, especially when alone, was exceedingly vulnerable to heightened emotional disturbance. This, he reasoned, could have a detrimental effect upon her maternal drive, and therefore such a woman could not be held fully responsible for her actions. A few years later, at the end of the eighteenth century, John Haslam, the Bethlem Hospital apothecary, made a study of eighty women who had been admitted to the institution suffering from insanity following the recent births of their babies. He asserted his claim that "menstruation, parturition, and... nutriment for the infant" were the principal contributory factors to female insanity. But it was not until 1820, when a leading London obstetrician, Dr Robert Gooch, published his treatise, *Observations on Puerperal Insanity*, that the first formal clinical assertion was made that childbirth could, and did, lead to insanity. He wrote:

> During that long process, or rather succession of processes, in which the sexual organs of the human female are employed in forming, lodging, expelling, and lastly feeding the offspring, there is no time at which the mind may not become disordered; but there are two periods at which this is chiefly liable to occur, the one soon after delivery when the body is sustaining the effects of labour, the other several months afterwards, when the body is sustaining the effects of nursing.

From this point forward an infrangible link was forged between the physical stresses of childbirth and the female psyche. The medical and legal professions in a sense colluded with one another, lending credence to the notion that giving birth was enough to make a sane woman mad. Within two years the condition detailed by Gooch was being cited in the defence of a woman on trial at the Old Bailey for the murder of her baby.

According to Joel Peter Eigen in his exhaustive survey of the evolution of the insanity plea, *Witnessing Insanity: Madness and Mad-Doctors in the English Court, 1760-1843* (1995), this was the first time a "gender-specific psycho-physiological debility" was entered in a defence plea. At the time much was made of the testimony of a surgeon, Joseph Dalton, who argued that the defendant, "an affectionate wife" and a mother who had previously demonstrated nothing but "correct parental feelings", had succumbed to the combined effects of a hereditary predisposition to insanity, the physical exertions incumbent upon the act of birth, and a "breast extremely full of milk", and had therefore, in a temporary derangement, murdered her baby.

Interestingly, this case predates the formulation of the McNaughton Rules, which state that a person cannot be held responsible for something they have done if they were "labouring under such a deficit of reason from disease of the mind as to not know the nature and quality of the act, or that if he did know it, that he did not know that what he was doing was wrong". In 1843 Daniel McNaughton shot and killed Prime Minister Peel's Private Secretary instead of his intended victim, the Prime Minister himself. His defence was that he was suffering from the delusion that the Conservative Party was trying to destroy him, and he was found not guilty by reason of insanity and committed to Bethlem. The ensuing debate in the House of Lords led to the formulation, in 1843, of the McNaughton Rules.

Even after this, however, insanity defences per se were rarely used in the case of mothers who had murdered their newborn children. In such cases there was a wholly different understanding, one which was, strictly speaking, against the letter of the law and founded upon little more than a common-sense approach to mental illness. From the 1840s up until 1922, as far as the judiciary was concerned, women "crazed" by the social, physical and mental stresses which pregnancy and childbirth often inflicted upon them were objects of pity who were either rendered utterly incapable of controlling their own actions, or were driven by an entirely rational desire to spare themselves and their families further descent into poverty and/or shame. It was their very contrast to "ordinary" murderers which was typically emphasised: their domesticity and devotion to their families, even, most touchingly, to their little victims. Needless to say, when poor working-class men acted under similar pressures and took the lives of their children, they rarely met with the same degree of sympathy.

By the mid-nineteenth century puerperal insanity and its related disorders, lactational insanity and insanity of pregnancy, were well-established medical conditions. In some studies it has been suggested that the diagnosis was applied to up to twenty five per cent of all female admissions to mental asylums: even conservative estimates place the figure at above ten per cent. Gooch characterised it as a condition that "may exist in any degree between mere peevishness and downright madness. Some women", he observed, "…are so irritable after delivery that their husbands cannot enter their bed-rooms without getting a certain lecture; others are thoroughly mad."

In 1846 John Conolly, the physician at Hanwell Lunatic Asylum in Middlesex, wrote an account of thirty-one case studies of puerperal insanity. He noted that poor women, particularly those with illegitimate children, were the social group most likely to be diagnosed as suffering from puerperal insanity, although "fashionable" women, he averred, were prone to the condition too (even the young Queen Victoria appears to have been a sufferer, "troubled with lowness" after the birth of her second child in 1841, and moved to observe that the process of childbirth was "indeed too hard and dreadful"). Conolly also classified the illness, identifying two main forms: the maniacal and the melancholic. The maniacal woman "sings, talks incoherently and laughs much; is sleepless, dancing, undressing herself, over-turning chairs, breaking windows, kneeling down and praying loudly, and sometimes manifesting sexual excitement". Her melancholic sister is, by comparison, listless and highly anxious about domestic affairs, continually reproaching herself for neglecting them. This understanding of the two most typical forms of puerperal insanity was to hold sway for the next seventy years.

By the time Beth gave birth to her babies in 1919 puerperal insanity was recognised in the International Classification on Diseases, and suicides resulting from such cases were entered as a valid cause of death under the category of "childbirth fatalities not assignable to other causes". John Fairbairn, in the 1921 edition of his *Practitioner's Encyclopaedia of Midwifery,* expounded what was by then the received wisdom, that "Maniacal Depressive Insanity....is frequently associated with childbirth". He advocated that the woman be presented with meals "tempting and artistically laid..." and that half an hour before eating such meals the patient "should take a dose of ...dilute nitrohydrochloric acid [a corrosive and highly toxic agent used for cleaning gold] and tincture of nux vomica [in which strychnine predominates] or decoction of cinchona bark [quinine]". Those who were refusing food "must be regularly tube fed" a mixture of four pints of milk and four eggs every day, and regulation of the bowels was also held to be very important.

By the time Fairbairn was writing, it was beginning to be understood that there may be some underlying psychological factor to puerperal insanity, as he put it, "some unconscious conflict respecting ideas of birth and sexuality". But this was still, in the early 1920s, cutting-edge thinking; for most of the nineteenth and early twentieth centuries it was widely believed that the condition was somehow due to the *physical* effects of pregnancy, childbirth and lactation. The Victorians had observed that the "stresses" and "demands", the inevitable exigencies of childbirth and rearing, produced insanity in some mothers; as one late nineteenth-century expert put it, "the reproductive act... is always and of necessity inimical to life...."

By 1919 it had long been accepted that women who endured a difficult labour, for instance, or one in which traumatic interventions have been made (such as forceps delivery, for example) were much more vulnerable to suffering from insanity than were others. It was also accepted that, in the words of one late nineteenth-century lecturer, women who had children in rapid succession became enfeebled, anaemic, hysterical and "the prey of... nervous maladies", with insanity occurring in about 0.25 per cent of all pregnancies, according to several contemporary authorities. The apprehension of poverty, morbid fear of ruin and loss of social status were widely recognised as constituent in a significant proportion of all cases, as was anxiety over the illness of children.

Victorian doctors also recognised that there was something particular about insanity of the puerperium, as compared to other forms of insanity. Its onset was always rapid and acute, with most attacks occurring within a fortnight of giving birth; it often produced acts of impulsive violence (usually directed at the baby); it was the only form of insanity (apart from some forms of acute delirium mania) accompanied by a raised temperature; and the sufferer was usually completely recovered within three months (although it was generally recommended that they should remain away from home until the baby was six months old).

By the end of the nineteenth century many doctors were advancing the idea that the cause lay in some form of sepsis. After birth the mother's body no longer had any need for most of the "pabulum", the nutrients the pregnant body had manufactured for the unborn child, and it was commonly believed that the presence of large quantities of decomposing septic matter inevitably led to systemic poisoning which, in turn, caused the insanity.

Early twentieth-century doctors did not, of course, have the same understanding of the endocrinal system as their late twentieth-century successors. In modern times there has been an unwillingness any longer to consider as axiomatic the relationship between motherhood and mental disturbance, but the understanding that puerperal psychosis has some underlying chemical cause has become widely accepted in recent decades. What we now know is that during pregnancy the levels of the hormones oestrogen and progesterone surge to between one hundred and one thousand times their normal levels. Then, within five days of giving birth, they drop back to their pre-pregnancy status. The resulting shock to the endocrinal system induces the spontaneous and unstoppable flood of tears that befalls three-quarters of all new mothers: the "baby blues". For some women the weepiness is literally uncontrollable and coincides with the "let-down" of the mammary glands, with the first gush of milk from the breasts.

For most women, the fluctuating desolation and euphoria will subside after a day or two, but for as many as ten per cent of all newly delivered mothers the baby blues will intensify into a prolonged bout of deep depression.

In real terms this means that of the six hundred thousand British women who will give birth in the next year, an astonishing sixty thousand of them are likely to suffer for at least the first six months of their babies' lives from full-blown PND (post-natal depression) – entry into a bleak landscape where irritability, fatigue, anxiety, sleeplessness, and loss of appetite, enjoyment and libido are the norm.

Of these depressed new mothers, up to five per cent will graduate from moderate to severe depressive illness, and some will become so ill that they will be referred to the psychiatric services and may even be admitted to a psychiatric ward. This includes a proportion of newly delivered mothers who will have developed chronic schizophrenia. In addition, in any given year there is always a number of women who have killed their babies, but who do not come to trial because they have also killed themselves. The Confidential Enquiry into Maternal Deaths, conducted under the auspices of several Royal Colleges in 2001, revealed that post-partum suicide is one of the highest causes of death in otherwise healthy young women.

The reasons why puerperal insanity occurs at all, in the course of what is after all a perfectly natural life experience, are still not entirely understood. The medical orthodoxy offers an array of underlying causes, most of which apply to all those diagnosed with depressive illnesses and are not at all peculiar to recently delivered women: an unhappy childhood and a problematic relationship with one's own parents, isolation, lack of support and especially the lack of a mother figure, feelings of conflict and doubt about the "trigger" situation, stress factors such as recent bereavement, divorce, moving house, poverty, unemployment, bad housing, intense disappointment, unresolved issues and emotions, feelings of anger and confusion. In other words, the stuff of life. Depressive illness on this telling can, and probably does, happen to each and every one of us at some time in our lives. But why is it that women who have just introduced another life into the world are among those most vulnerable to its wheedling, insidious progress?

There is some scientific evidence that certain people may have a hereditary vulnerability or genetic sensitivity to fluctuations in those hormones which affect mood. It has been known for thirty years now that oestrogen, along with other steroid hormones, influences the serotonin transporters in the regions of the brain which play an important role in the affective functions.

The amygdale, for example, which plays some role in the operation of the emotions, and the hypothalamus, involved in the sex and sleep drives, are normally rich in serotonin, but levels of the "feel-good" hormone are depleted in all people suffering from depression. There are other theories and possible contributory factors. Some women develop a thyroid condition after pregnancy which causes them to be lethargic and overweight. These physical conditions can themselves give rise to negative states of mind, and depression, which are in turn exacerbated by the drop in serotonin that is another by-product of thyroid under-activity.

There is recent evidence that for a great many women the experience of childbirth is in itself such a negative one that it can lead to Post Traumatic Stress Disorder (PTSD). This is particularly true in those birth experiences where interventions, such as forceps, drugs to speed up labour, or caesarean section, have been made. The symptoms of PTSD were first diagnosed in men returning from the Vietnam War, although shellshock was of course recognised during World War One when thousands of men returned from the Front with the tell-tale NYDP ("Not Yet Diagnosed Psychiatric") on their official records. Sufferers typically experience intense panic and anxiety attacks, flashbacks, recurrent nightmares, an inability to relax, emotional detachment from others and reduced libido. These symptoms and variants of them are still present in many cases twelve months after the initial trigger experience, but there are some people who suffer for years.

7

"Yes mum, no mum"

Beth's childhood in Potterspury, already docked with the cares of family life, was brought to an abrupt end when she turned thirteen. After that age it was no longer possible, when a fine day came along, to take a picnic up to the Queens oak tree in Yardley Gobion and to sit under its shade with her lace. The time had passed when she could run through the fields of buttercups until her boots turned yellow with their dust. No more skating on the lake at Grafton on frost-spangled nights. She was too old, now, to join the other kids in the chase after the racegoers on their way back from Towcester, cadging pennies from the lucky punters, or to go with the Sunday-school class to take tea in the Coach House of nearby Wakefield Lodge, the seat of the Duke of Grafton.

In October 1891, having just brought in his last-ever harvest, Lou's father, Sam, died aged 76 from the cumulative effects of "old age, diarrhoea and exhaustion". His entry in the census of April 1891 describes him as "Pauper – Ag Lab", as if the two were synonymous. He was one of thousands of prematurely aged men, bent double by the time they were fifty from long hours spent working in the fields, dressed in clothes that were always damp. He was also a loved father and grandfather, and one of the last links to the old familiar ways and places. He would have found it hard to imagine his grandchildren and great-grandchildren, and their descendents scattered far and wide, like poppies across a great meadow, growing up well beyond the small cluster of villages he and his forefathers had rarely if ever ventured outside. The changes witnessed in their lifetime baffled old countrymen of Sam's generation. One was interviewed by the social surveyor Benjamin Seebohm Rowntree in 1911, and posed the rhetorical question many must have grappled with: "What was the land sent for if it weren't for the poor to live off of?"

Lou had no choice, not if she wanted to spare her mother the final indignity of ending her days at Buckingham workhouse, but to take Sam's relict, Martha, into the little cottage in Potterspury. There was just enough room now that the two older children were already out of the house. The eldest son, Herbert, was a shoe-riveter lodging with a stitchman and his wife in the village of Stanwick a few miles away. The eldest girl, Julia, was in service in the home of a Cornish builder and his Northamptonshire-born wife in Willesden, north-west London. So that left just four of them, Martha aged sixteen, Beth aged twelve,

Evie aged ten and six-year-old Ernie, to share the one room with their aged grandparent. Beth would now have to leave off school in order to help bring in some extra money.

Her older sister, Martha, had been living with Lou's parents in Leckhampstead on and off since the Tamworth days, and had been bright enough to earn the post of assistant teacher in the village school. In fact she had just taken her candidate exam when her grandfather fell ill, and she had to give up on her plans for work. That first tentative upwards move for the family was now dashed, and poor Martha found work at the post office in Yardley Gobion stamping envelopes instead. There was no choice in the matter. A certified teacher could have earned more than £90 a year (equivalent to about £6000 today and roughly twice what Joe brought in), but the fees for the training still had to be found. As a pupil-teacher (one of the few careers open to girls in the late nineteenth century) Martha's earnings would have been little more than a few shillings a week, even less than could be earned making lace. Moreover, training at a pupil-teacher centre took three years, and with it came none of the benefits of domestic service, which took care of the girl's board and lodgings and left more money to be sent home. However much Joe and Lou might have yearned for respectability, they simply could not afford the luxury of deferred gratification.

One contemporary guide to suitable employment for young women discusses the problems faced by the daughter of a "labouring man", such as Martha, who becomes a pupil-teacher. Such a girl "is educated – not cultivated", the author informs us, "and the work of learning thoroughly, and teaching well, must be essentially foreign to her ordinary home-life." Though condescending, this observation probably held true for Beth and her sisters. It would have been an exceptional Victorian working man, even one like Joe, with his literacy and high regard for books, who was able to appreciate the worth of an educated daughter. There is always a kind of diffidence to be overcome in poor families. A sort of fear sets in which prevents the head ever being lifted high enough to scan the wider horizon; it is a profound fear of anything beyond the known, the set patterns of existence, which have after all ensured the survival of the family thus far. Beth's family had tried once before to enter the unknown, and they knew better than most that to do so was to face the possibility of failure and ruin.

Beth, for her part, was spared the pangs of thwarted ambition experienced by clever Martha. Firstly, it was generally the sickly daughters of the poor who took to pupil-teaching, if they were able, those who were too delicate for the rigours of life in service or too unhealthy to make an attractive match for a labourer or tradesman. Beth was little and skinny, but she was not "waukly", as they used to say in Northamptonshire. Also pupil-teachers were required to have "clear and clerk-like" handwriting in order to pass their certificate, and Beth's handwriting and punctuation (though not her spelling which, once her illegible "artistic" scrawl has been deciphered, proves to be of a high order indeed) bears all the marks of someone whose schooling has been little more than adequate. Beth was never under any illusions: she had been brought up to work, and if you are brought up to work, so they say, then work comes easy to you.

However, even for a sensible, hard-working and capable country girl like Beth, there were very few employment opportunities in nineteenth-century rural England, so it was likely that before long she would have to go to the town, as Joe and Lou had tried to do before she was born, and where her oldest sister Julia now found herself. There was at least some chance there of making a life for oneself. Factory work was one option, but it would have been an abhorrent choice in a family which had been laid so low by the incursions of the machine processes. The only labour Beth had been trained for was lace-making, but only a fool would allow their daughter to follow that trade by the 1890s. Many country girls took up some form of hawking in the towns and cities, especially in the dairy, flower or fruit trades, but Joe and Lou would not have entertained such a career for one of their daughters. The only other sources of gainful employment for young working-class girls were prostitution and domestic service. The first, though potentially lucrative, was plainly out of the question and so, at thirteen, Beth left off school altogether and went into service.

She started as a day-girl in the village, still living at home but going off each day to help the wife of a local tradesman, who, though clearly no "better", was mystifyingly "better-off" than her own father was. From seven o'clock in the morning until around six or seven o'clock in the evening she joined the nearly two million other women who spent their days helping wealthier women to keep their homes, a daily course she was to follow for the next ten years.

Beth still had her dreams, though. A neat and skilful needlewoman, she was later to confide that she had once thought of becoming a lady milliner, keeping her own atelier where rich ladies would visit in search of a pretty little bonnet or eye-catching tocque. Unfortunately for Beth, such a dream was even more outlandish than were her sister's teaching ambitions. Lady milliners were usually gentlewomen, not the daughters of humble village tradesmen. And even if Beth had managed to overcome that particular social hurdle, there was no way she could have amassed the capital necessary in order to set up a business of her own. Nor could she ever have afforded the fees that established lady milliners charged their apprentices; these ranged from ten to thirty guineas, the equivalent of up to nine months wages for her father.

***

Lou's aged mother, Martha, lived on for two years after losing Sam, increasingly senile, and almost completely blind after her long years of lace-making, eventually dying in her dutiful daughter's arms. There is a small but telling record of the effect the loss of both her parents had upon Lou. In the time between registering her dad's death and her mother's she has completely forgotten how to sign her own name, marking the second certificate with an "X". Less than a year later she received another blow: Joe suffered a stroke and lost the power of speech. He had kept working just long enough to see the family he and Lou raised together begin their independent lives. When Joe became an invalid, after more than forty years at the last, only one of his children, eleven-year-old Ernie, was still living at home. Lou was to nurse Joe for three years before he died. During that time he became increasingly helpless, and she was wracked with the bronchitis that would eventually kill her: the effect, no doubt, of inhaling the charcoal fumes from her warming-pot, exacerbated by the years of living in a light industrial workshop.

Luckily for Joe and Lou, all their children were by then settled in good positions, and able to send money home. Indeed the couple would have been entirely dependent upon their support. Without it, even a good hand such as Joe could find himself staring disaster in the face within a very short space of time, should he have the misfortune to fall ill. The four bob a day he had previously brought home would not be replaced by anything else. If he got behind with the rent, he and his wife would first have the few sticks of furniture they owned taken away, and within a couple of weeks they would very likely be homeless. This was the common fate of many respectable, hard-working independent tradesmen. Apart from the workhouse, there were very few options available to such people: in larger towns there were cheap lodgings where a room could be had for a few pence a night, but the society there would be too dreadful for a refined craftsman, who now only had his pride. It was possible to find furnished rooms, rented by the day for a shilling, but the only way of raising such a sum would be through pawning clothing, boots, wedding rings and, eventually, the man's tool-kit. Once the tools had gone into hock there really was no going back: you can't turn a penny without tools. In the last three years of their life together, Joe and Lou would have eked out a meagre living from what their children could send them, subsisting on penn'orths of tea, twists of sugar and slices of bread and butter, as Joe declined into speechlessness, confusion and depression.

By the time Joe died in 1899, Beth, now twenty-one, was far away from Potterspury. Perhaps she was glad to have distanced herself from the confinements of the cottage, her weak and weary mother, the spectacle of her once proud father laid so low, and the village, lace-making, and every-thing that her parents and grandparents had taken for granted.

Perhaps she felt homesick from time to time, worried about her poor ailing mum, and cried when she thought of her dad. Or guilty at the ease with which she had managed to shuffle off the past and find a certain satisfaction in her new life. But these were subjects one did not touch upon in general conversation.

***

Entry into the homes of the better-off, even though she was just a servant girl, gave Beth something she could aspire to, something that was perhaps more easily attainable than a little millinery shop. When her family had gone to church in Potterspury, they would have been accustomed to the spectacle of Augustus Charles Lennox FitzRoy, the 7th Duke of Grafton, entering through the chancel door, and his entire household (more than fifty servants to attend to the needs of seven or eight members of the duke's family) entering through the main one. They must have been an impressive sight: the footmen, especially chosen for their good looks and height, handsomely attired in livery, the frock-coated butlers, the maids in their smart black dress-es and stiff white caps and aprons.

Many of Beth's neighbours and childhood friends went on to take up positions in the Duke's household, which was one of the mainstays of local employment. But Beth's route out of rural poverty was to be a little less intimidating. After a year or so spent as a day-girl in the village, she went to work for the Gibberds – Mr Gibberd, a successful boot wholesaler (a business contact of Joe's), his wife, Lillie, and young daughter, Freda, who lived in what was then the leafy Surrey suburb of Upper Norwood, close to the Crystal Palace. Theirs was precisely the type of comfortable, lower-middle class home that Beth could easily have imagined acquiring for herself one day.

During her time at the Gibberds, Beth became "Lizzie", a name nobody in my family can ever remember her using before or since. Her father was always careful to enter her full name, "Elizabeth Annie", on any documents, and certainly her sisters called her Beth later in life, as did everyone else. But when he filled in the 1901 census, Mr Gibberd put her down as "Lizzie" (which made it difficult for me to find her on the index until I had the brainwave of looking for the Gibberds instead). Eventually a char was employed to help with the really dirty jobs and Lizzie became elevated to the status of cook/domestic, but for most of the eight years she spent with the family she did everything about the house that Mrs Gibberd did not have the time or inclination to do herself. It was frequently said in the country that hard working, capable, trustworthy girls like Lizzie – those who were anxious to make a good impression – made the best wives. It was while in the employ of the Gibberds that Lizzie developed into a gifted cook, and if you could do good plain-cooking in addition to all those other attributes, then you had everything a man in the same situation as yourself could possibly wish for.

Lizzie would have cooked lunch for her mistress and the family when she was a day-girl back in Potterspury, and she would also have been expected to help her mother when still at home, but in the Gibberds' service she had the money to spend on more varied, good quality ingredients and a talent began to emerge. Beth's cooking was still being talked about, in near mythic terms, years after she was no longer there to serve up her hashed beef and batter pudding with a few crisp greens on the side; pink and juicy boiled bacon, fried potato and buttery carrots; fat bloaters, turned in a little Worcester sauce and oozing with piquant juices; pneumatic steak and kidney puddings; chunky mince and glistening onions in lustrous gravy; sherry trifle made with hedgerow fruits, shimmering jelly and her own sponge cake crumbled into creamy custard.

Apart from the opportunity to develop a skill, domestic service also provided Lizzie with a role model. Mrs Gibberd was not so different to the girl herself in terms of social background, and was only a few years older, but she was able to teach by example the best way to make a steady progress towards respectability and the lower rungs of the middle classes. Mrs Gibberd's home had a bathroom (something Lizzie would never have) and proper beds (this would have been the first time Lizzie had ever slept in one of her own) made up with good linen all tucked in just so, flounced with valances and topped with layers of blankets and quilts – not with overcoats and jackets, like at home. Mrs Gibberd liked the table to be laid properly with side-plates, napkins and three sets of gleaming cutlery. Lou might well have known how in an ideal world these things should be done, but she never had enough room to lay out a proper table, and anyway back home in Potterspury there was barely enough cutlery and crockery for everyone to have just one of each. Lou had perhaps a few good family pieces, but these were never used at the table; they sat on the plain shelf above the fireplace. Now Lizzie found herself in a home filled with hand-embroidered table linen, fish knives, lead crystal glasses, and with a dresser bedecked with matching patterned china. Like all aspirant Victorians, Mrs Gibberd would have filled her home with possessions which she hoped would display her social standing: dark landscapes and suitably moral themes hanging from the picture rails, flock wallpaper, densely decorated rugs overlying densely decorated carpets, a piano in the parlour, a sewing-machine, charming ornaments on the decorative overmantel, heavy brocade and lace in every window, tallboys with Chinese bowls atop them which overflowed with aspidistras. Her memory of the Gibberds' home was a template for all the homes Beth was to make throughout the rest of her life.

Mrs Gibberd probably influenced Lizzie in another way, too. She had only one child, Freda, who was ten years old when Lizzie left the family's service. I have no idea why the Gibberds had only one baby when other families of their time had so many. A great many aspirant lower-middle-class couples of their generation certainly made use of contraceptives, but there were also many others who saw it as a mark of their success to have huge broods of healthy, well-turned-out children. Whatever the explanations as to why Freda remained an only child, it is likely that Mrs

Gibberd educated Lizzie (who most likely started her periods around the time she went to work for the family) about the facts of life, and that Lizzie learnt from her example. Surely, in comparing her mother's life with that of Mrs Gibberd's, she must have seen how much easier it was for a woman who had somehow managed to avoid the demands of a large family.

Mrs Gibberd wanted things to be done in a certain way, but there is no indication that she was a harsh mistress. In fact, Lizzie seems to have derived an enormous amount of self-esteem from her valued role in her mistress's life, and her successful career as "Cookie" is one of the few things about her which has been passed down with a discernible pride.

There is even some reason to suppose that the two women became very fond of each other – close, even. Lizzie also appears to have been very fond of little Freda. Years later she would pass on the child's name to one of her own. "Lizzie" was bustling, good-natured and hard-working, but "Beth" was lonely and homesick, missing her mum, and her sisters Martha and Evie (they remained close through their lives) and the rough-and-tumble and spontaneous affection of life in a large family. No doubt Freda filled a big gaping hole in the life of the young servant girl: she was someone little to love and play with, to take care of. Many young servant girls formed deep emotional attachments to the children in their care. Some of them even suffered nervous collapse after leaving the service of families where they had grown especially close to the children they had helped to raise.

Tony Ward, Principal Lecturer in Law at De Montfort University, and an expert on the legal history of infanticide cases, has charted the case of a nanny, who, in 1923 after a row with the mistress of the house and under threat of dismissal, locked herself in the kitchen with the family's four-year-old and ten-month-old daughters and turned on the gas. The nanny was found in a coma, but the two little girls were dead. In her defence the nanny alleged that she was driven to murder by intense feelings of maternal love for the older girl ("I am taking my darling Sonia with me, I know she would not be happy without me", ran the suicide note she left), and equally intense hatred towards the child's natural mother.

But Lizzie was not given to any peculiarities of nature, not at this stage anyway. She carried out the bulk of her work every morning, neatly attired in her print dress and plain pinafore. She appeared smart as a new pin in the afternoon, in her navy-blue and fancy apron – with a neat little cap on her head – opening the front door to greet Mrs Gibberd's "company" with a curt bob. She was always the first to rise in the house, leaving her bed at half-past five every morning to start the range, and then carrying tins of hot water upstairs for the family's baths, and a jug for Mr Gibberd to shave with. Then she set about preparing and setting the breakfast, and then washing-up after the family had eaten it. Next she applied herself to turning out the bedrooms, followed by the hall, the dining room, the parlour, the bathroom, the kitchen and the scullery.

This all had to be accomplished by midday, when Lizzie had to be ready to serve up the dinner she had prepared: ham and eggs, brown soup, tansy and spinach pudding, salads of garden lettuce, cucumber and tomatoes; carrying the dishes to and from the table, followed by more washing-up. In the afternoon there would be silver to clean, or rugs to beat, linen to smooth, and windows to rub clean with newspaper and vinegar. A flurry of baking: fruit cake, scones, bread, tarts and pies, sponges for tea. Then the supper to be laid out: croquettes of carrot and bacon, a baked cod's head or a thick-collared trout, stout veal and ham pies. And that was how the days of Lizzie's youth slipped by.

Mrs Gibberd might lend a hand if there was anything extra, but otherwise it was all left to Beth. There was a routine devised by the mistress, with a day for everything: Mondays and Tuesdays – bedrooms; Wednesdays – the downstairs rooms; Thursdays and Fridays – the kitchen and the kitchenette. The time passed in a bustle of brooms and scrubbing brushes; hands reddened and roughened from the effects of Condy's fluid and ammonia. There were oily rags for polishing the brass (a real chore in the damp weather when no matter how hard you rub it won't keep bright) and elbow grease and spit on the iron to check if it was hot enough. Finally, when it was all cleared away – hopefully by eight o'clock – there was a little time to yourself. Time to do some sewing or knitting, to read one of your stories lying on the bed in your own little room. Time to dream about the future: of life in her own home, with her own girl to help her, a handsome husband, not itinerant like her poor Pa, but successful – a dealer, like Mr Gibberd, or a shopkeeper perhaps, a baker, butcher or greengrocer...

8

Young man waiting in the refreshment bar of a large rail-
way station: **I say, could you oblige me with a match?**
Good-looking girl with red hair presiding over said bar:
Yes, if you do not mind it being a red-headed one.
From *How to Be Happy in Marriage* by Rev E.J Hardy, 1901

Even today, more than sixty years after it burnt down
in a final spectacular conflagration (viewed from as
far away as Brighton, sixty miles to the south), Upper
Norwood is still dominated by the architectural wonder
that was the Crystal Palace. The avenues and thorough-
fares of the entire suburb, laid out with views of it in mind,
are still haunted by the spectre of Paxton's magnificent
confection of glass and wood. Walk along the Parade, past
the bus terminus, and there is an eerie sense that something
is missing; travel north along Church Road, where Beth
and the Gibberds lived, and it is as if there is a great hole
in the skyline. The Phoenix TV mast tower (which stands
over seven hundred feet tall on the former site of the

Palace) provides a focal spot on the broad horizon, but it does not explain the residual energy that still hangs in the air over Sydenham Hill.

Visible for miles around, the proto-theme park of Victorian England occupied an area six times the size of St Paul's Cathedral: thirty-three million cubic feet encased in five hundred tons of wrought iron, three and a half thousand tons of cast iron, nine hundred thousand feet of glass, six hundred thousand feet of wooden flooring, thirty miles of gutters. The central transept alone, just one of three, was over one hundred feet high, and contained a vast avenue and upstairs galleries which ran for hundreds of feet. On every day (except that is, thanks to the Lord's Day Observance Society, for Sunday) thousands of people would come to walk around the enormous glass-frame galleries stuffed with examples of Egyptian, Roman, Renaissance, Chinese and Grecian statuary and architecture. They could visit Pugin's approximation of a medieval court, stroll around the vast grounds with their gargantuan waterfalls, thrill to the spectacle of Benjamin Waterhouse Hawkins's life-sized models of dinosaurs (installed on their own specially manufactured island), or sit in the enormous four thousand-seater concert hall and listen to the Great Organ, with its four thousand, five hundred pipes. On many occasions, in the period between 1899 and 1901 when they were courting, Beth and her paramour, Bertie Wood, would have been found there amongst the throng.

Church Road leads up to the point known as the Crystal Palace Triangle, and it was there that the huge south transept of the building and the art school it housed stood, until it burnt down in 1936. The Gibberds' home, at number 56, stood in a new and smart terrace of shops and houses not far from the junction with Crystal Palace Parade, and just a short walk from Fox Hill (still recognisable as the charming snow scene painted by Pissarro). Today this top end of Church Road is very run-down, but at the turn of the last century the whole area was at the centre of a prosperous suburb, with few signs that the slow, steady downturn in its fortunes was already beginning.

From the top of the road Beth would have had a good view of the South Tower, one of the two immense brick water towers built by Isambard Kingdom Brunel in order to store the millions of gallons of water needed for the Palace's water fountains. The towers dominated the area until they were demolished at the start of World War Two, but even in the late 1890s the supreme national confidence which had summoned up the Palace forty years before was waning. At the end of July, 1899, Beth and Bertie may well have witnessed the reactivation of the fountains, which had been out of use all year, and joined the thousands of others taking a turn about the grass terraces in front of the Palace, to marvel at the great jets of water, shooting two hundred feet in the air. But the excitement was short-lived, and within a few more years the fountains would be rusty from lack of use and neglect, and the great water basins which housed them entirely grassed over. Today, wandering across the grassy slopes, a visitor may encounter a lone sphinx covered in graffiti, or come across a flight of stone steps abandoned in the middle of the yearning space. But you will search in vain for any other signs that the Palace was ever there.

Beth would have done most of the shopping on Westow Hill, a busy street at the junction of Crystal Palace Parade, with a butcher's, dairy, stationer's, pharmacy, and a florist (which Zola photographed during his stay on Church Road, in 1898-99, when his involvement in the Dreyfus Affair forced him out of France). For fruit and veg, though, she would have taken a little detour away from the high street, walking up Woodland Road and then turning left on to Woodland Hill. There, about two hundred yards along, were the greengrocers, Pettley and Wood, situated on the ground floor of a well-appointed double-fronted red-brick house (now gone).

The business was established sometime before 1871 by Bert's maternal grandfather, Daniel Pettley, who used to stand in the doorway dressed in a bowler hat and a white apron. He had arrived in Norwood when the suburb was still being laid out, and cannily set up shop just behind the railway, a few minutes walk from the Palace itself, then in its heyday. Before coming there, Dan Pettley had been a farmer's bailiff, hailing from Latchingdon in Essex, one of a generally hated breed. Bailiffs were often characterised as hard men, who rode about the manor, lording it over the labourers, screwing up rents and screwing down livings, and generally doing the dirty work of estate managers and landowners. They tended to be chosen from outside the areas they worked, in a deliberate strategy to prevent compassion for erstwhile friends and relations. Dan, however, had served as bailiff on the very estate whose fields he himself had once worked, and where his father and other relations continued to labour. When he moved his family to Sydenham in the 1860s he left behind an aged mother who died alone, a pauper. The Pettleys were not the type to allow sentiment to hinder ambition.

Bailiffs were also frequently accused of feathering their own nests by both cheating their masters and exploiting the labourers. Perhaps this was how the family had managed to garner enough money to set up a greengrocery business in such a good area. They were by all accounts very shrewd and quick-witted. In the Middle Ages the Pettley ancestors had owned a great deal of land around Orpington, in Kent, and during the fifteenth and sixteenth centuries had sued and countersued one another over numerous property and inheritance rights. By the eighteenth century Dan's branch of the family (always spelling their name with two "T"s, even though few of them could read and write) were reduced to working on the land rather than owning and squabbling over it. Dan Pettley might have done all right for an illiterate peasant, but when he stood up on Sydenham Hill and looked across at the magnificent views to the south, he was looking down on land that at one time might well have been his birthright. I wonder if this was something he was ever aware of, and if this was the knowledge which drove him?

His business acumen was considerable. Like Beth's dad, Joe, had attempted to do, he had moved his family miles away from their home at great risk, having spotted an opportunity. He opened his shop in a good position, knowing that he was assured custom from the numerous day-trippers and the very nice class of people who had been attracted to the fine mansions being built along the spacious wide avenues, with their splendid views up to the hilltop Palace. The business Dan Pettley founded flourished for almost thirty years. And after he died suddenly following a fall on the pavement outside the shop, its continued success for the next ten years was almost entirely due to the hard work and determination of his youngest daughter, Bert's mother, Ellen.

Nineteenth-century shopkeepers' daughters, it is often said, set the fashions in a district, but it is very hard to accept this was ever true of Ellen. Family photos of her show a formidably visaged, uni-bosomed woman, her hair scraped back off her decidedly spud-like face. But whatever her physical shortcomings, Ellen knew how many beans make five. She was hard-working, clever (the only one involved in the business who could read and write) and determined to make all the right connections: to scrimp, save, and what ever else it would take, in order to nudge herself and her children up the social ladder. But none of this made her a nice person. My uncle remembers as a small boy watching with horror as Ellen, his great-grandmother, then in her late seventies, whacked a gardener across the back with her walking-stick because he had missed some weeds in between the ornamental stones on her front path. Even when she was an old woman, the family remained in her thrall, and grown men took pains to avoid crossing her. There was only one person who was never afraid of her and that was her daughter-in-law, Beth.

When they first met, Beth might well have been impressed by the shrewd businesswoman, who clearly revelled in the power which running a shop gave her. Standing at the doorway in her pinafores, with a calico money belt around her stout middle, Ellen must have been a rare instance of a self-assured, unyielding woman, in charge of her own business and her family's destiny. As a mother-in-law, however, she was of an entirely different order.

Ellen was a terrible snob who enjoyed passing judgment on her customers, ingratiating herself with those of good class, and telling the poorer ones what they could and could not buy. She relished the sway she had over the more desperate of her customers, granting the right to buy on tick to those she reckoned would pay her back and refusing others outright. She rarely made a wrong decision, and rapidly totted up the bills on her fingers, licking them to mark the tally. Shops were the social centres of Victorian and Edwardian England, and Ellen (along with her mother who helped in the shop until she died well into her nineties) heard all the gossip, even while they sternly admonished the gossipers. The gossip gave her the information she needed to carry on her business: somebody's son had just found work on the omnibuses, so they could be relied upon to pay their bill; somebody else was drinking too much, so their slate would need to be paid off as a matter of urgency. There would have been very little that went on in Upper Norwood that Ellen did not make it her business to know about, and few of her customers escaped her gimlet eye and unerring ability to size up a person.

Ellen had a husband, William Wood, a rough giant of a man with the speech and manners of a costermonger, who greeted customers with his shirtsleeves rolled up to his elbows, revealing his huge bulging forearms. He was somewhat rougher than Ellen perhaps would have liked, and not altogether steady, but he was as indefatigable as she was in pursuit of an income. He rose at the crack of dawn every day in order to drive the dray-cart down to Covent Garden to buy the stock (a fourteen-mile round trip); although, lacking his wife's head for figures, what he bought was always to her order. He would arrange the vegetables in boxes, set at an angle, in the big front window, and the fruit in pyramids on top of the barrels outside on the pavement, but he did so under her watchful eye. He placed the signs "Home and Empire", "Produce in Season", "Apples 6d 1lb", but only Ellen was capable of writing them out. In short, his name might have been over the door, but William Wood merely helped the missus to run the shop.

As far as Ellen was concerned her choice of marriage partner was a further impediment to her advance through society. When she had married him in 1876, William Wood had been an illiterate labourer and the son of an illiterate labourer. He must have had some hidden charm, because it is not immediately apparent from the fragments of evidence that have survived what else he had to offer the ambitious young Essex girl who was so dedicated to upward mobility. In fact, the origins of the Wood family in Norwood are very obscure. There are very few records of them in the parish register before the appearance in the 1830s of William's father Thomas, a road digger who was employed in 1854 as a navvy on the excavations and construction of the Sydenham site, when the Crystal Palace was moved there from Hyde Park after the Great Exhibition of 1851.

Family legend has it that before this time they had been travellers, who had earned their keep by horse-dealing, and who had only lately emerged from the dense woods which had once covered most of Norwood and Penge. It is almost impossible to prove this either one way or the other, but there were certainly gypsies in Norwood: their presence has been well-documented since the seventeenth century, and it is often said that to look into the eyes of a Norwood local is to look into the eyes of a gypsy. By the 1830s at least one writer was referring to the "olden times", when the "nut-brown gypsy pitched his camp under the shades" of Norwood's forest, and so it is possible that the Woods were part of the resulting diaspora.

Gypsies or not, what is known is that they were involved in the horse trade. A great facility with horses was one of the principal qualities of my grandfather's paternal family (some might say it was their only quality), and my grandfather knew a great deal not only about horses, but also about travelling people and their ways. I have a strong and clear memory of being taken to a fair with him when a very small child and being introduced to an old crone who lived in a traditional wooden caravan, beautifully decorated inside and out. I can remember my grandfather lifting me up into it and him talking with the old lady for a long time, and I was impressed by the familiarity and ease between them, especially because I found her rather strange and more than a little frightening. Travelling people were part of his life, of course, as he toured the fairgrounds of Britain trying to sell his novelty hats, but it was always clear that the showmen liked him, and even held him in a certain regard. Whenever we accompanied him on these trips my sister and I would be treated to free toffee apples and free rides. Once, we were given a free coconut when the man on the shy refused to let me have a go, out of respect for my grandfather, and took me round the back of the shy to show me the little wedges of wood which made it impossible to dislodge all but one of the nuts.

Bert was Ellen and William Wood's oldest son. He certainly played his part in the family business, helping in the shop and delivering orders in his donkey dray, but he and his dad and younger brother spent a lot of the day involved in other spots of business. They were "higglers", dedicated to earning whatever extra cash they could by more or less whatever means presented themselves. Chiefly, though, they were on the lookout for anyone who had in mind a "swop" of a horse, mule or donkey. They lived for the big horse fairs, especially Barnet, where there was no such thing as a quiet sale. Thousands thronged about, as the Wood men conducted their business in a cacophony of whistles and shouts, concluded with a slap of hands and the loud declaration of the agreed purchase price ("Four pahnd ten, mate!"), followed by general rejoicing in the quick sale and exchange of horse flesh.

Bert and Beth were about twenty when they started courting. She probably set her eyes on him as he served her in the shop, and maybe they cemented their relationship when he came to call at Church Road in order to deliver her order. In company with other couples, they would stroll around the Palace, occasionally taking the chance to thrill to Ronco and Monte's strongman act, or have a laugh at the humorous lectures of Arthur Helmore. No doubt they took the Reno Inclined Elevator from the terraced grounds to the upper galleries of the Palace, and marvelled at the "animated pictures" of the Boer War. Beth was always interested in whatever was going on, and maintained a lively interest in everything new until her old age. She and Bert would have taken their tea and cakes in the Café Chantant and looked at the lovely views across Surrey and the Kent downs, stretching far into the distance.

Perhaps once or twice they stayed out late to see the stupendous fireworks, set off at 9 o'clock every Thursday night, when the entire spread of the sky around the building would be illuminated. One recreated the bombardment of the Alexandria forts; another a flight of twenty monster dragon flies. Afterwards, Bert would walk Beth back to the Gibberds' house on Church Road, see her safely indoors, and then turn up his collar and walk home alone.

How could they not have become infused with the glamour and excitement of the Crystal Palace? How could they not have fallen in love? They had to take care, though, all the same, for Ellen had her eye on the little redhead, and had her own view as to whether a "domestic" was ever likely to be good enough for her eldest son.

In their old age, which is all anyone alive now can remember of them, Bert was Beth's physical opposite: she was titchy, spry and skinny, but he lumbered like a great ox, his huge square head bolted straight onto his broad shoulders, his hands like spades. His leathery skin was as brown as a nut, and the aroma of pipe tobacco hung all around him, and in the space he had previously occupied long after he had gone. He had a voracious appetite his whole life. I imagine he, like my grandfather, loved doorsteps of white bread slavered with thick dripping and mustard. (My grandmother, against her better judgment it has to be said, kept the dripping in a crock by the stove; "peasant food" she called it, disdainfully). Their idea of a good meal was a plate of well-done sausages and gravy or chops and gravy, or mince and potatoes swimming in gravy. The gravy always sopped up with another enormous chunk of bread which they pushed around the plate with a fork, only just stopping short of licking it clean.

Bert was, like his own dad, very strong. He once stunned a bull that had gone berserk in Romford market: having steered it into a yard, he jumped onto its back and punched it several times between the eyes until the raging beast sank to its knees. But he was a quiet and acquiescent man who had been henpecked into submission by his mother long before Beth stepped in. Bert knew the names of every leaf, bird and insect in the forest, and was never known to harm any of them. He would do anything for a quiet life and, apart from his spindly little wife and his children, he loved nothing so much as his pipe and the pint he had each evening after his dinner.

Much of this is gleaned from the memories of my mother and her brother, though of course they only knew him during the 1930s and 1940s, when he was already in late middle-age. Back when Beth (as he always called her) first clapped eyes on him some time in the late 1890s she would have seen a sweet-natured (perhaps even biddable), but nonetheless virile young scion of a comparatively successful family who she had every reason to suppose would one day inherit a well-established greengrocer's business in a comfortable London suburb. He must have seemed a really good catch.

She had no father now, of course, to introduce Bert to, only the weary and homely Lou. Joe, even in reduced and straightened circumstances, might have impressed a prospective husband and his family had he still been alive, but not Lou, installed in her humble little cottage with everything all very plain and worn out, her widow's black by now threadbare and quite rusty with age, coughing and coughing. No doubt Beth consulted Mrs Gibberd (who probably knew the formidable Ellen; after all they were both the wives of successful local tradesmen, even though Mrs Wood dirtied her hands a little more than Mrs Gibberd would have been prepared to do). Perhaps Mrs Gibberd even allowed the young swain to come and sit with Beth one evening a week, once they were engaged of course, so she could keep an eye on the mismatched couple: the energetic, little redhead and the gentle, lardy jobernowl she had set her cap at.

Any dreams which Beth may have had of becoming the wife of a respectable tradesman were, however, short-lived. For by the time Beth and Bert started courting, he and his dad were already preparing to move on from the fruit and veg; they had in mind other, less onerous, means of earning a few bob. By the turn of 1901, as the nation mourned the death of Queen Victoria and the Prince of Wales was preparing to give his name to a new, exciting era, these other ways and means were proving so lucrative that for the Woods the early morning starts driving the dray-cart to Covent Garden would soon be a thing of the past.

***

On the 9th October 1899 the South African Republic issued an ultimatum to erstwhile shoemaker's apprentice Joe Chamberlain, Colonial Secretary in Salisbury's government. The Republic demanded the immediate withdrawal of all the British troops currently on her borders and the recall of all reinforcements sent to South Africa since the previous June. Chamberlain, bent on a ruthlessly imperialist policy in the Transvaal, rejected the ultimatum and so, on October 12 1899, burghers of the South African Republic and the Orange Free State invaded British "uitlander" settlements at Cape Colony and Natal.

The Second Boer War of 1899-1902 has been called "the last gentleman's war", but in reality it was a dark and shameful episode, founded upon the ruthless pursuit of world domination by a nation at the zenith of her imperialist power and determined to be the sole possessor of Transvaal gold. The war presaged the horrors of twentieth-century warfare and, spanning as it did the last years of Victoria's reign and the beginning of the Edwardian era, ushered in a modern sensibility. It cost the lives of twenty thousand Imperial and Colonial forces, many of them as a result of disease and incompetence in the carriage and supply of rations.

The "guerrilla" tactics of the Boers, their surprise attacks with rapid-fire German Mauser rifles, their superior knowledge of the terrain, gave the uniformless and ill-disciplined rabble a distinct advantage over the might of the Imperial and Colonial forces during the first months of the conflict. Forced to cross vast sections of the Veldt in poor quality clothing (apart, that is, from their stout Raunds-made boots!) that managed to be inadequate against both the boiling heat of day and the freezing cold of night, in constant fear of a courageous enemy who had nothing to lose and all to gain, the British were in a precarious situation for most of the first year. But after Lords Roberts and Kitchener took command in 1900, the war entered an eighteen-month period of ruthless suppression of the Boers.

Three thousand miles of barbed-wire fence was thrown up and grim stone blockhouses set at every hundred yards. Into these compounds the Boer women and children were herded, as their homes and farms were burnt to the ground. The concentration camp had come into being. By the end of 1901 more than hundred thousand people were interned in the camps and more than twenty thousand of them, the majority of them children, would die painful, lingering deaths as a direct result of the squalid conditions and severe food shortages imposed upon them.

There were frequent antiwar protests, especially when Emily Hobhouse and the Women and Children's Distress Fund brought the suffering of the Boer women and children to the public eye, and a great deal of controversy over the mounting cost of the war (more than £200 million in total). But chiefly the war gave rise to a huge wave of patriotism in Britain. Men flocked to join up, the music halls ringed with rousing jingoistic choruses, and the Reliefs of Mafeking and Ladysmith were celebrated amid scenes of mass jubilation. Altogether half a million men served in the Boer War, in the wake of a massive recruitment drive.

I have no idea whether Bert tried to do his bit by going into uniform. I do know that he volunteered for the Front in World War One, but was turned down on the grounds that the work he was doing was more valuable to the war effort, and it is entirely possible that the same objection was made in 1899. The work Bert and his father and at least two of his father's brothers were engaged in was horse-dealing.

Horse-dealing was the second-hand car trade of the nineteenth and early twentieth century. There was a huge market: in London alone there were more than three hundred thousand horses in the 1890s, and there were fairs all over the country where men could make money buying and selling horses. One of the biggest was at Smithfield in London, which was held every Friday afternoon and lasted for three hours. According to family legend, Bert and his dad were well-known characters at the race tracks too.

Most horses in circulation were at least second-hand and a great many of them were third-, fourth- or fifth-hand. There was a huge demand for sturdy beasts to pull the carriages, dray-carts, hansoms, coaches, omnibuses and dog-carts that conveyed the Victorians about. First, horses were sold by the breeders as yearlings to grazers who fattened them up for a couple of years before passing them onto farmers, where they were broken in and worked until they were about five or six years old. Then they were sold on to dealers who in turn passed them on to whoever was interested, took them back, and sold them on again until the poor beasts were only fit for the knackers. Then there was more money to be made selling the worn-out carcass on for glue and dog- and cat-meat, the origin of the expression "going to the dogs".

A dealer with a well-formed horse, with good hock and knee action, standing between fifteen or sixteen hands high and weighing 1100-1400lbs, could name his price. Unfortunately, many of the horses on the market were as far-removed from this ideal as it is possible to be: they were lame, balky, spavined, broken-winded and moon-blind. The dealer had to employ a panoply of tricks of the trade in order to pass them off as a good buy to the unsuspecting.

The secrets of the "gyp" horse dealers were guarded zealously and passed from father to son. My grandfather knew an awful lot of them, learned as a boy when he helped his dad and uncle in the trade. He knew how to fatten up a poor quality horse with treacle and milk; and how to paint on youth spots, dye white hairs, trim and singe manes and tails, so that even the beast's previous owner could be duped into buying a horse he had just sold on. He knew how to place a blanket to disguise a sway back; how to temporarily lessen lameness by pouring boiling turps into the sole of the troubled foot; how to treat a spavin (a bony tumour that grows on the legs of some horses); which teeth to pull to make a horse look younger.

This was the secret knowledge my grandfather carried with him, and which he occasionally let slip (once he astounded my uncle by calming a startled mare they encountered in the street, gently walking her into the horsebox to the relief and approbation of her groom who had failed to still her). It was also yet one more area of his life about which he could feel ashamed. Firstly, he loved all animals and must have hated being involved in what was often a cruel trade. But secondly, he was very ashamed of such a close connection with such a low-class and despised business which often bordered on the criminal. He once confessed to my uncle that he had hated his time during the First World War walking strings of horses down to Tilbury Docks where cavalry officers loaded them on to boats bound for the Front, mainly because he had been taught a crafty way of counting the legs which was designed to dupe the quartermasters into thinking they were buying more steeds than they actually were. As a young impressionable boy, living through the vainglory and trumpeting that characterised the Great War, he had found this sleight of hand a wholly unpatriotic practice and one which, in his mind, irrevocably tainted him.

More than three hundred and fifty thousand horses and fifty thousand mules died in the dust and heat of Africa during the Boer War (in one episode of the conflict, the Siege of Ladysmith, the Imperial Forces were so hungry they had no choice but to eat their own mounts), so the total numbers of horses involved in the war must have been many times that. There was evidently a great deal of money to be made by canny men who knew how to supply the need. The thoroughbred Irish hunters were the most sought after, the equivalent today of a good make of saloon car with "one careful previous owner", but they were thin on the ground and at this stage in the war the army could not afford to be choosy. A sturdy five-pound scrubber would do just as well as a well-boned mount, for all that was required was that the horse was strong enough to take a twelve-stone cavalryman and his saddle and equipment. The prices paid ranged from £12 for a fifteen-hand high cob, up to £40 for a "hairy" hunter: the lower figure is the equivalent of two months wages for a working man at the turn of the last century. The Woods must have been coining it in. In February 1901 the War Office despatched thirty thousand more troops, most of them mounted, and a couple of months later Bert's family shut up the greengrocer's shop forever and moved out of London. They had set their sights on the market town of Romford in Essex, a centre of the horse trade with its own knackers' yard, surrounded by grazing land and conveniently close to the docks.

And they took Beth with them.

9

"Married people who are fond of each other spare one another a lot of irksome and harrowing little details."

Daily Mirror article, 1901

A large cattle market was held each week in Romford from the thirteenth century (when Henry III granted the right to the town), until 1958 (the year after Beth died). On market days horses would be led through the centre of the town to be sold and the local gypsies would emerge from their dwellings in the remnants of the old Hainault Forest a few miles to the north. For centuries, on Wednesdays, the route into Romford from the north, through Epping Forest, would be thronging with horses and dealers, all making their way across what is now the busy Eastern Avenue intersection (also known as the A12), and following the line of the River Rom down to Market Place itself. Until the 1920s the route the dealers followed, and the area, as far as the London Road to the west, was still mostly fields filled with grazing horses.

Like Beth's home-town, Potterspury, Romford stands on one of the old Roman Roads, actually the military route linking London to the fort at Colchester; its situation on a major thoroughfare had assured the town a steady and lucrative stream of traffic from its earliest days. The opening of the Southend Arterial Road, in March 1925, encouraged expansion and development in the land around Romford, and before long it was no longer possible to walk a short distance out of the town in any direction and find yourself standing in open countryside.

When Beth and Bert arrived there in 1901 the town was already beginning a period of exponential growth: it had doubled in size in just twenty years and was, by then, home to almost twenty thousand people. The town clerk was predicting that the population would double again by the end of the decade; in fact, by the time of the 1906 General Election, the Romford Division had become the largest constituency in the country, with sixty-one thousand people. There was plenty of building land and a fast train connection, and in May 1901 the town was connected to the telephone system. But although rapidly emerging as a modern urban entity, Romford was still just small enough to conquer, and almost big enough to hide away in if all went wrong.

In amongst the embryonic modernisation and burgeoning civic pride, remnants of the old, dark world could still be discerned. There was much poverty and hardship in the rural hinterland that edged the town. Soon after the Woods arrived, a pea-picker gave birth in a ditch and another threatened to cut the throat of a rival in love. Gypsies living on the edge of the recently laid out Mawneys housing estate (built on the site of an old manor house) were regularly in trouble for cruelty to horses, for stealing wood and clothes from the workhouse and for stealing eggs. And among the desperately poor inhabitants of the town itself there were many social problems: child neglect was an all too common feature of the local court reports, as were sexual immorality and drunkenness (or "excitement", as the local paper preferred to call it).

Ellen must have spotted the advertisement in the March 22nd, 1901 edition of the *Romford Times*, because she was the only one in the family who had enough smarts to know where to look and what to look for (and she was also the only one who could read well enough).

...A charming Freehold Country Residence standing in its own grounds of about 1/3 of an acre, with stables and coach house; containing ten rooms, bathroom and the usual domestic offices. Excellent state of repair. Price £1500.

The house was Cottons, built in the eighteenth century by a wealthy local family. It was a fine Georgian pile, complete with drive and portico, and it stood at the top of London Road, right by where Waterloo Road joins the High Street, and the point at which, one hundred years ago, the flat farmlands of rural Essex gave way momentarily to the smoking chimneys of the brewery and the bustle of the market town. Nowadays all that remains of the fine house where my grandfather was born is the Cottons Recreation Ground, opened in the 1920s after the council bought the fifteen acres of land on which the house once stood for £25 an acre (close to £1000 at today's reckoning). Most of the rest of the land which once surrounded the house, and presumably the foundations of the house itself, today lies under the huge roundabout that links local routes to the A12 which curls around the north end of the town before dropping down to Southend.

Cottons had undoubtedly been a splendid house and afforded all the Woods (including Beth) an inspiring glimpse into the promised riches of the world. Small wonder, then, that my grandfather, who never owned his own home and died in a council flat, always gave the impression that life had somehow cheated him and that he had been born for better things.

Whether Beth went to Cottons as the family cook or as the fiancée of the eldest son and heir is unclear. Family legend has it that the couple were secretly involved, and came up with a ruse whereby Beth would come into the service of the Woods with the understanding that in due course Bert would pluck up the courage to tell his parents about their relationship. But it seems to me unlikely that Beth would have taken such a gamble, trading a good post, one where she was happy and secure, in order to throw her lot in with Bert on the strength of a slender promise. In their relationship, Beth always had the upper hand. It is possible that she made the move to Romford as cook, in the secret hope that she would be able to seduce the son and win round the rest of the family, but again that seems out of character – too risky and melodramatic a scheme for Beth.

Whatever the circumstances, the young couple were married very quickly, within two or three months of their arrival in Romford, at St Andrew's Church (opposite Cottons) on July 7th, 1901. This, it seems to me, was no shot-gun affair (my grandfather was born a hair's-breadth the right side of respectability almost exactly nine months later), but the predictable conclusion of a courtship which had been conducted for a couple of years or so and with the knowledge and apparent acceptance of the groom's family. On the certificate Beth does not give an occupation, which she might well have done if she were until very recentl, employed as the family cook. Either way, by the time of the wedding both bride and groom had already been "living tally" at Cottons for a good few weeks.

Mrs Gibberd was present at the wedding and she, along with Bert's mother, brother and sister, has signed the register. Her presence demonstrates how close Beth and her erstwhile employer had become, but what are we to make of the proliferation of Wood signatories? Family legend has it that the Woods were angry about the marriage, considering it a great shame that their eldest son and heir should have thrown himself away on a cook. Certainly

Beth never believed that the marriage had the blessing of her mother-in-law. However, Bert always remained close to his mother and brother and Beth, although she disliked old Mrs Wood and tolerated Bert's brother Alf, liked his sister, Maud. Was signing the register some sort of peace-offering, a symbol of the willingness of all parties to let bygones be bygones? And is there any significance in the apparent absence of any of Beth's family as signatories? Were they unhappy with the union Beth had arranged for herself? Or did Beth think that Mrs Gibberd was more deserving of the honour of signing her wedding certificate than was her old mum (who in any case had difficulty with writing, and might have only been capable of leaving a shaming mark on the register rather than a signature)? Perhaps none of her brothers and sisters could afford the journey to Romford; perhaps Lou was too ill as well as too poor to come. I have looked at Bert and Beth's wedding certificate countless times and each time I come away with a different impression of how things were on that July day. Sometimes these pieces of paper, these slivers of information that survive the years, raise far more questions than they answer.

Whatever the circumstances of the marriage, it seems that once Beth was installed in Cottons she began to claim that she was the object of her mother-in-law's slights. It is around this period that the first symptoms of Beth's "awkwardness" begin to emerge. It is always difficult to live with the in-laws, even in a large house such as Cottons. In Mrs Gibberd's house Beth had an assured status and a valued role to perform, but in Cottons she had to fit in with the Wood tribe and, in particular, fall in line with her mother-in-law's every decree. To add to the stress of the situation, Beth spent most of that first year pregnant with my grandfather, far from anything familiar.

Her life had changed quickly and dramatically. The older woman ran everyone and everything, but Beth was not someone who could easily snap to it. Mrs Wood was a harridan, but Beth was proud and feisty. She was also young (just twenty-three), vulnerable, sensitive, and perhaps, too, more than a little defensive. I can hear her responding to the slightest criticism with the retort that she had been running a quality household for several years now without any complaint from Mrs Gibberd. She knew how things should be done, from what pictures to hang on the wall, to whether antimacassars were the last word in respectability or an old-fashioned encumbrance. But she was no longer "the help"; she was married to the eldest son and expecting his baby whether her mother-in-law liked it or not. And what is more she knew that she was just as good as the Woods, if not better. Her father had been no common higgler, little better than a gyppo horse-trader: he had been a master boot and shoemaker, and he had known how to write his own name.

The slights suffered at the hands of her mother-in-law, whether real or imagined, were never to be forgotten by Beth. Years later, after all that had happened, Beth would take delivery of churns of milk sent down from the big house (no longer Cottons by then), where her mother-in-law lived with Bert's younger brother, only to pour the contents down the drain in the backyard. My grandmother for one was very shocked by such wicked wastefulness: what about the poor kids living up the road, she implored Beth (by then her mother-in-law), or the legions of unemployed men to be found out begging on the streets? Or even the sick babies in the infirmary? Surely Beth should take the milk to them if she had no use for it herself. But Beth was implacable and her answer always the same: "I wouldn't give them [meaning her husband's family] the satisfaction..."

***

Lou passed away at the end of February 1902, from a combination of acute bronchitis and heart trouble. She was only sixty, but was worn out by years of hardship and anxiety. Since Joe's death her home had been a little five-roomed cottage situated on the road between Potterspury and Stony Stratford. Living with her at the time of her death were Beth's sisters, Martha and Evie, Evie's husband, Beth's youngest brother, Ernie (who registered their mother's death, aged just sixteen) and a female lodger to help with the rent. "Taking in lodgers" was always a safe resort when the squeeze was on. Lou had made the same calculation many poor widow women did, working out that there were some advantages to taking on a slightly larger property provided that grown-up children could be relied upon and a respectable lodger could be found to help with the increased rent.

The loss of her mother must have been a great blow to Beth, and more keenly felt when, less than a month later, she gave birth to her first child, my grandfather. No woman can ever be adequately prepared for the physical and emotional shock of childbirth, and every woman believes that her experience is to some extent unique, but for Beth, far from home and the comforting presence of her own kinswomen, it must have been a traumatic event.

Many of those who, like Beth, left their home villages at fourteen or fifteen to work in service in other parts of the country may not have even started menstruating when they did so; plenty of others went into their first labour not knowing what was happening to them. Children like Beth who grew up in the country over one hundred years ago had little formal schooling and certainly received nothing in the way of "sex education": they learned the facts of life almost without realising. They came out to cheer when a stallion was "walked" in an area, his mane plaited and dressed with ribbons, where he was to be "attended" by local mares. They knew why the cow was taken to the bull, the ewe to the ram; they saw the bees buzzing around the hedgerow flowers; came across dead lambs in the fields; gathered jars of frog spawn from the ponds and ditches. Perhaps when a little older, like Arabella in *Jude the Obscure*, they carried a bird's egg next to their bosom because "it is natural for a woman to want to bring live things into the world", and maybe like her, they even threw a pig's "pizzle" at a boy they liked. When people left the villages for the city (and by the early 1900s more than four-fifths of the population were city dwellers, as opposed to less than half fifty years before) they began to drift into ignorance about the natural processes they had previously taken for granted. For women in particular this immense change signalled an egregious loss of control over those forces which governed their lives.

Until the advent of the National Health Service in 1948, most women gave birth in their own homes. In 1902, when Beth became a mother for the first time, it was still the case that the majority would be attended by midwives (who were professionalised that year) rather than, as Queen Victoria had once referred to them, "those nasty doctors". In the past the midwives would be assisted by the woman's female relatives, usually her mother or a married sister, but, with the great dispersal of families away from their home villages into the towns this was becoming less common. Beth (along with many other women of her class and generation) was doubtless one of the first women in her ancestral line to have her first baby far from the parental home, and with no mother, aunt, grandmother or sister in the room with her.

Although there had been some improvements, childbirth was still fraught with many dangers one hundred years ago. At the end of the nineteenth century thousands of women still died in childbirth or as a result of perinatal diseases every year, and it was the highest cause of mortality in young females. In fact there is some evidence that the incidence of maternal death had actually risen in the previous decade, in spite of numerous advances in hygiene and birthing procedures. This was largely due to the increase in urbanisation and the poverty that nearly always accompanied it; life in the country was in general much healthier. The loss of support networks also contributed significantly to the extra stresses and privations poor women, newly moved to the cities, experienced in their confinements.

Beth was a very small woman, something which concerned early twentieth-century obstetrics, so much of which still held fast to the "old wives'" school of thought. It was axiomatic that confinements go "very hard" with little women, and there was a great fear that the baby's head would be injured as it tried to force its way through the narrow birth canal. The possibility of producing an "imbecile" in such circumstances haunted many women.

Caesareans had been performed successfully since the mid-nineteenth century, although there was a high-risk factor attached to the procedure. In the early part of the twentieth century there was an increased tendency for obstetricians to use "tools", such as forceps. It was often reported that one could tell just by walking past their beds which women in an infirmary had undergone such a delivery; in the days before routine episiotomy, most of them would have suffered some degree of vesico-vaginal fistulae (that is tears to the wall between the vagina and bladder) leading to continuous leakage of urine and an unmistakable odour. However, such interventions could only be made by a qualified doctor, and as far as Beth was concerned she preferred to be delivered by a midwife, as did most women given the choice.

This was often a decision made solely on the grounds of expense: a doctor would charge at least one guinea to attend a confinement (although in city slums many came to a woman in distress for a nominal fee of 10/6d), whereas a midwife could be procured for just 7/6d. But the real reason why so many women opted for delivery by a midwife was that they felt more comfortable with a woman delivering them.

Interestingly, then as now the incidence of obstetric complications and fatalities was in direct correlation to the presence of doctors in the birthing room. It had been observed back in the 1840s that women delivered by a doctor or medical student were far more likely to contract puerperal fever than if they were delivered by a midwife. In some of the lying-in hospitals (where the very poor tended to give birth, as public provision was made for the cost) outbreaks of puerperal fever accounted for thousands of deaths throughout the nineteenth century, often totalling five times the national average. The reason for this was long thought to be due to the "combustible" nature of newly delivered women, but in fact it had much more to do with their doctors' lack of basic hygiene. Male doctors were far more likely to "take pains", that is conduct internal examinations in order to deduce how dilated a labouring woman was, than were midwives, who could tell just by looking. Until Lister's work on antisepsis in surgery was accepted, after its publication in 1868, very few doctors bothered to wash their hands. They went from examining infectious patients, and even corpses, to conducting intimate probes of the maternal cases in their care, with no idea of the germs they might be spreading.

Even after doctors had learnt to wash their hands before delivering babies (until well into the twentieth century, in fact), women were still safer in the care of a midwife. This may have been because they felt safer and were consequently more relaxed. Modesty, too, was a big consideration for women who had been brought up to believe that nudity was shameful and that anything sexual was offensive. The idea that one would have to expose one's privates to a man, even a qualified professional, was unthinkable to the majority of women of all social classes. (Bear in mind that at the turn of the last century there were only about one hundred qualified lady doctors in the whole of the UK.) In the 1860s a West End consultant obstetrician, Dr James Edmonds (who had performed one of the few successful caesareans of the time), began to campaign for a class of "lady-midwives" in order to spare those "delicate-minded" ladies the terrible ordeal of an immoral encounter with a male doctor. Childbirth manuals of the time make great efforts to allay these anxieties, reassuring their readers that "taking a pain is done entirely by touch with the finger, and does not require exposure of the person in any way". But they do not address the concern that a man would be there as a labouring woman involuntarily vacated her bowels or peed herself. This shaming probability, which understandably concerns many women today, was perhaps the chief unspoken reason why the majority opted for delivery by a midwife, whatever fears they may have had as to the medical hazards of the birth itself.

As we shall see, the Romford midwife, Mrs Bennett, who delivered my grandfather, was extremely good at her job. She had been in practice for more than twenty years by the time she attended Beth, and combined large amounts of instinctive common sense with more than a smattering of knowledge of the modern advances made during her time in obstetrics. She was one of the first practising midwives to register when the 1902 Midwives Act came into force, which suggests a degree of professionalism and seriousness. Midwives were often unfairly characterised as more "Sairey Gamp" (Dickens's grotesque comic caricature of a fat, drunken midwife in *Martin Chuzzlewit*) than Florence Nightingale, but they were often in reality far more skilful than such a stereotype implies. It is true that (even after registration came into effect) there were thousands of illiterate old girls who combined midwifery with laying out the dead and dispensing herbal remedies, and who would happily perform either task for a few bob and a mug of gin, but even in many of those cases most midwives had years of experience in delivering babies. They also had expertise in all medical matters connected to childbed, and an array of practical skills and abundant common sense. They were expected to assist mothers with household duties as well as the birth itself, and the Midwives Board's professional standards placed as much emphasis on housewifery skills as upon personal hygiene and medical knowledge.

Early twentieth-century childbirth manuals frequently extol the wonders of the "modern age" and the great advances in medical science that had been made over the previous decades. Yet they describe a world in which, to our eyes very little appears to have changed in the practice and methods of childbirth in the preceding years. In most of them comparatively little attention is given to the actual birth, instead the writers concentrate on the preparation for birth: the imbibing of oxalate of cerium to combat the effects of morning sickness and syrup of figs to prevent constipation; the application of hot fomentations of permanganate of potash to reduce the symptoms of piles; the sewing and knitting of the layette. Many poor people made cribs from banana crates which could be bought for a penny, or from the bottom drawers of cupboards, and a lot of attention is given to how these contrivances might be made clean and comfortable with yards of valencing and calico and lengths of ribbon. There are lengthy descriptions of the numerous cleaning rituals of early labour in which mothers were expected to play a significant role.

Perhaps women derived some comfort from these preparations, which would certainly "take your mind off" the impending event.

The manuals devote page after page to the importance of cleaning the floors and walls of the lying-in room; wiping the bedposts down with disinfectant; making protective coverings for the mattress; putting out the baby's clothes to air; setting bedside tables with jugs of boiled water and rolls of clean cotton binding and all the other paraphernalia of childbed: slabs of carbolic, bottles of Condy's Fluid, blunt scissors, Vaseline in pomatum jars. The midwife would provide her own bottle of little coloured pellets of biniodide of mercury, used to make up a hand-washing solution, keeping them in her pocket so that the deadly poison could not find its way into the wrong hands. A labouring woman of Beth's generation could expect to receive a glycerine enema, have her privates shaved and her vagina and nipples swabbed with weak solutions of carbolic acid as preparation for the moment of birth itself.

In the great majority of those books written before World War One it is generally assumed that most babies will be born to women in their own homes, with minimal intervention. The use of chloroform in labour had been pioneered by Queen Victoria, but it was not administered as a matter of course, and midwives were not qualified to use it unless under a doctor's supervision. The chief labour pain-management device of the nineteenth and early twentieth centuries was a roller-towel attached to the foot of the bed, usually at the right side. The labouring woman could find relief "during the pains by pressing her feet against the bottom-right-hand corner of the bed and pulling upon it". In addition a dose of ergot could be administered, if the midwife considered it necessary, and another of laudanum once the birth was over.

Throughout her ordeal the drinking of beef tea and, in extremis, brandy was encouraged in order to keep up the spirits of the labouring woman. Women were expected to restrain themselves, to hold their breath and "refrain from crying out": any feral displays would, they were assured, only make the pain worse. They spent most of their labour lying on their right side with their knees pulled up (often justified as a means of ensuring modesty in the presence of a doctor). They generally gave birth with their buttocks positioned on the edge of the bed, so that those minister-ing to them could support them without having to stretch too far.

Fathers were permitted to attend a birth, if the couple so wished, but in most manuals it is quite clear from the tone that this was not to be encouraged. In reality most men were banished from the lying-in room or, more likely, chose to stay well away until all the necessary and unpleas-ant business had been attended to. Once safely delivered, babies were to be put to the breast immediately, not (as now) to ensure bonding, but in order to prevent the occurrence of breast abscesses. Newly delivered women were typically advised to "try and control their minds" by restoring "strength to the body and richness to the blood", partaking of fresh air and "cheerful company", keeping their bowels regular with aloe and myrrh pills, and being very careful "to have only a moderate amount of sexual connection", in the words of one contemporary manual.

A minimum convalescence of nine days was recommended if it could be managed. A great many women looked forward to their post-natal confinement as one of the few opportunities for a rest in their fraught lives, even if they often spent it sitting up in bed darning socks and kneading bread in between bouts of nursing. But in poor families the mother's continued incapacity often spelt ruin, as husbands failed to do the shopping within the meagre budgets their wives were so adept at stretching. Women felt compelled to leave their beds as quickly as possible, so worried were they by the prospect of dirty homes, hungry kids and dwindling financial resources. These were the women who doctors considered most at risk of suffering mental collapse, specifically "lactational insanity", induced by anxiety, poor diet and exhaustion, exacerbated by the demands of breast-feeding.

* * *

For Beth, once the fearsome ordeal of childbirth was over, she might have been expected to settle back and enjoy the rest and attention. After all, life at Cottons was relatively comfortable, and she had produced a healthy baby boy upon whom she doted. But it appears that things did not proceed at all smoothly. The loss of her mother, the continued strained relationship with her in-laws and the pressures of first-time maternity were perhaps bound to precipitate some crisis or other. The continuing downturn in family relations coincided with a sudden diminishment in the Wood's fortunes over the first year of my grandfather's life. In May 1902, as Beth made her first tentative adjustments to motherhood, the Treaty of Vereeniging was signed, bringing to a conclusion the second Boer War, the Boer republics of Transvaal and the Orange Free State, and with them the great boom in the horse trade. A few weeks later a man was fined for driving his motor vehicle at 25mph through Romford. The horse trade would continue for a while yet, but even a fool could tell that its days were numbered.

In response, Bert took up poultry dealing, a fad at the time in the London suburbs where eggs were expensive and hard to come by, and the keeping of chickens discouraged on hygiene grounds. Unfortunately, Bert could not make eggs pay. The Woods tried keeping a few cows, along with the horses, on the grazing land opposite Cottons, but the milk trade was much more vulnerable to competition than was the horse trade with its zealously-guarded secrets that only a few were party to, and it was not the money-spinner they hoped for. The Woods were adaptable and canny, but it slowly began to dawn on them that they had probably had the best of the feast.

As far as Beth was concerned, the modest dream of being a respectable tradesman's wife was fading fast. She found herself locked in, for better or worse, with a good-natured but somewhat beef-brained husband who was completely under the thumb of his mother. The first flush of married love began to give way to a whole host of rather more negative feelings: insecurity, irritability, resentment, tinged perhaps with a little self-pity and depression. She began to be critical about her life and her surroundings, and to express a fear that circumstances were beyond her control. This is the period in which she began to acquire her reputation as a difficult woman, and long after she had gone it was still being said about her that "she could be very awkward". Years later she would talk about her profound sense of "disappointment" during this period of her life, and the feeling that she had been let down. She began to feel "very low, just very low" a great deal of the time and, although she adored her darling Reggie, her belief that her mother-in-law "looked down" on her, and the indignation that belief engendered, threatened to spoil everything. She could not bear to be the object of "that woman's" scorn, and any conciliatory effort the older woman made, offers to help with the baby for example, simply fanned the fires of Beth's resentment. Eventually either Beth or Bert (but more likely it was her) could stand it no more. When the spring came in 1903, shortly before my grandfather's first birthday, the little family left Romford without so much as a by-your-leave.

***

Bert had exchanged one dominant woman, his mother, for another, Beth. Even those in the family who took her part observed how "she must have led him a terrible life". Beth was cleverer than Bert, and she could be forceful to the point of obdurateness, bossy and nagging. He for his part would do anything for a quiet life. So it was at Beth's instigation that the little family went to Stony Stratford, the market town just a short distance along Watling Street from Beth's childhood home, and set in the same part of the Ouse Valley where some of her siblings were still living. Her younger sister, Evie (to whom Beth remained very close all her life), and little brother, Ernie, were living along with Evie's husband in Cosgrove, just three miles away across the Northamptonshire border. Her older sister Martha, now married to Tom, a local boy lately returned from the Boer War (whom the sisters had known since childhood), was settled in Stony itself. The sisters were in close contact with one another, and they would all have been familiar with the town. This was where their dad had brought his boots to market, and where Lou and her mother had come to buy from the pin-maker in Bull's Yard.

Stony Stratford is still a very pretty and relatively unspoilt town, with picturesque Georgian shop fronts and medieval inns. Thanks to its situation on the main road to London and the North, it had been a main thoroughfare since the Middle Ages, resounding to the rumble and thunder of coaches pulled by four horses, and the blast of the coachman's horn. Now it is entirely by-passed due to the proximity of the M1, a process begun in the 1870s when the development of railway works at Wolverton, a mile or so to the north-east of the town, began Stony's transformation from busy coaching halt to sleepy backwater. When Bert and Beth came to live there grass was growing long in corners of the once bustling market place. In addition to the railway works there was also a boat works, and during my grandfather's boyhood the High Street was enlivened from time to time, as the large vessels built there were towed by steam engines to the wharf at Old Stratford. From there they were launched on to the Grand Junction Canal a short distance away.

Bert and Beth set up home at the north end of the High Street, close to where the river Ouse winds around the town, an area vulnerable to occasional flooding. Bert found work as a labourer at the railway works and they settled to their life, concentrating their efforts on raising my grandfather who in due course was sent to the Church of England school in the town. For the next few years they had virtually no contact with the family in Romford. During that time Cottons was sold, almost at a loss, and Bert's parents went to live in a rather less grand home (a newly built mansion block behind the market on Laurie Square) which they rented rather than owned. It was left to Bert's younger brother to salvage what remained of the family fortune, and this he did by steadily building up a contracting business founded upon his ownership of a couple of strong shire horses and a big dray cart. He started by carrying out household removals, and ferrying goods up and down the London Road and down to the docks at Tilbury. Eventually he would own a great pantechnicon emblazoned with his name, and a home almost as grand as Cottons must once have been.

Bert's life had undergone an immense change. Beth was used to a life of hard work, and she had faced the possibility of ruin since childhood. She was happy to be away from her mother-in-law's whip hand, and back on home ground. She wanted to be "steady"; to avoid worry and uncertainty. In Stony she knew "up was up" and "down was down", she had her two sisters close by and all was familiar and safe-seeming. Poor Bert, on the other hand, had only known life as the eldest son of a comparatively successful and comfortably off tradesman. He was a cheap John, a bagman, who had grown accustomed to the fruits of a bit of wheeling and dealing; now he was reduced to having to work for a living, told what to do, a wage slave, occupying a place little above that of his own navvying paternal grandfather.

He had to rise each morning at dawn and walk to the railway works a couple of miles away. There was an electric tramline running between Stony Stratford and Wolverton (furnished by what were the biggest cars ever to run through a British town), but it cost 2d just to make the journey one way. Bert only earned eighteen bob a week, and he handed everything over to Beth. In return she gave him a shilling, just enough to cover his ale and baccy. He was not about to waste any of it on tram fares and besides, he could cycle faster. Sometimes it seemed as if his pipe was all he had to call his own, and it would have been considered strange if he had not joined the rest of the station men at one or other of Stratford's pubs on a Saturday night: "everyone" went along (the takings on such occasions were regularly in excess of £100) and it gave him something to look forward to during the long tedium of his working week.

Bert may have been dispirited and missing his old life, and the excitement of the fairs and racetracks, but he certainly did all he could to please Beth and to take care of his little family. He grew vegetables in a glass frame out in the yard, some of which went on the family table and the rest he took to work with him to be sold at the station. He also kept a pig and a couple of chickens; he knew how to butcher and he made a bit extra on selling the eggs.

Beth would have been quite pleased with what he brought in, and satisfied that he did not have to resort to the odd bit of "snobbing" old boots, or tinkering burnt and broken pots like so many of his co-workers did. For her part, she managed the money he gave her very well. She saw to it that the rent of 2/6d was paid, that there was coal in the grate, candles, oil for the lamps, soap and washing soda, and food on the table. Beth would stretch the money by making lard, black pudding and chitterlings when Bert slaughtered the pig; she would rustle up glistening batter pudding and crunchy roast potatoes with the joint on a Sunday; currant puddings were made with the fruit from the garden and lashed with custard made from the hen's eggs; an occasional rabbit stew would be made to last for a couple of days; and in heavy weeks treacle and rice and bread and marge would help to fill the distance between one pay-day and the next.

Beth might have given up on hopes for the grand life, but since her days with Mrs Gibberd she knew how things were supposed to be done and she was not going to keep a poor little hovel as her mother had had to do. The five-roomed terraced house was her first proper home, and she was determined to make something of it. The extra bed-room could be used from time to time to give lodgings to family members and those recommended to her: the extra from the rents would come in handy. She knew that there were certain items which were essential if a family were to stay the right side of respecta-bility: a kitchen fender and a nice set of fire-irons, oilcloth for the floors, a sofa, a hard-wood armchair for Bert to sit in, in front of the fire, with a nice cloth hearth-rug at his feet; four kitchen chairs and a sturdy table; a brass-mounted bedstead, a mattress and flock bolster; a washstand with a tile splashback. (I am not sure if Bert and Beth ever had a piano in their tiny parlour, but my grandfather could certainly play and when he was a grown man he kept a room filled with two pianos and a pianola.)

These items were bought out of money saved by Beth during her time at Mrs Gibberd's, and when that was all spent, saved for out of whatever was left after Bert and the boy had been fed and clothed. She had most of these precious items in use in her home for fifty years. It must have looked as if life was actually rather settled and contented. She might have even allowed herself a little sigh of relief from time to time.

Beth was able to manage so well because she was eminently practical and hard-working, but it was also down to the fact that she had just the one child to take care of. Mothers of only children often faced the resentment of their female neighbours and relatives who found that as soon as one little trouble was over another was beginning. But Beth, never one to gossip herself, ignored the tendency in others. My grandfather basked in her adoration, and was unchallenged by any sibling rivals for five whole years.

The memory of those happy days left him with a great affection for Stony Stratford. (It was the destination of some happy family outings with him in my own childhood.) I have a photograph of him from the Stony days, aged about seven or eight, taken with his class under the stern gaze of a heavily moustachioed master and a bored female teacher. He stands out from the other children, not just because he is immediately recognisable and so unmistakably a nascent image of his older self: he looks so clean and well-turned-out, resplendent in an Eton collar and dickey bow. I know he was happy there. And yet when I look at this image of his boyhood self I wonder if I am the only one to notice the weary expression, more befitting a grown man than a small boy and already bearing the traces of the deep anxiety that would dog him all his life. If I had been his mother it would have worried me to see it. But of course by then, by the time the picture was taken, he was no longer the only one in her life.

10

"Can we any longer wonder why so many married working women are in the lunatic asylums today?"
From a letter sent to Margaret Llewellyn Davies, of the Woman's Co-operative Guild, by an anonymous working-class wife and mother, 1914

In 1909, the BMA carried out a survey of the so-called "Secret Remedies", which purported to cure disorders of the "female sexual instinct". The survey found that there were no less than thirty-nine different proprietary brands of "female medicines" on the market. It appeared that in a short space of time numerous enterprising individuals had spotted an opportunity: a female population desperate for guidance and help, dispersed far away from their village wise-woman, and the networks they had previously depended upon for guidance and support and instruction. Mrs Arons's Women's Remedies were "made by a woman for women" and promised to "remove the irregularities and barriers which trouble young, unmarried women", and to "strengthen and invigorate the sexual organs of women of mature years in the change of life and those of barren women". Nurse Powell's Corrective Pills and Widow Welch's Female Pills, to name just a couple of examples, pledged to remove all "obstructions" and "blockages", and in densely worded descriptions, carried widely in the tabloids and women's papers of the time, guaranteed "to bring relief".

Coming across these advertisements a modern reader might think they were innocent cures for constipation, and smile on calling to mind an elderly female relative's obsession with bowel movements. The adverts were, in fact, covertly phrased advertisements for abortifacients, usually made of oil of pennyroyal or quinine, which women were taking in an effort to "restore" their periods to "regularity". But ridding themselves of unwanted babies was not the only concern of Edwardian women, and not the only condition to which they sought a remedy.

Sociologists and social campaigners of the early twentieth century, such as Seebohm Rowntree and Maud Pember Reeves, gave many ordinary wives and mothers a chance to speak for themselves probably for the first time and, although they weren't especially looking, their findings reveal that most of these women presented with symptoms nowadays identified in the DSM-III-R (the Diagnostic & Statistical Manual of Mental Disorders).

Maud Pember Reeves's 1913 study, *Round About a Pound a Week*, found many of her working-class subjects to be silent, passive, undemonstrative and unable to imagine more than "the same surroundings with a little more money, a little more security and a little less to do..."

A similarly overwhelming hopelessness resounds through Margaret L Davies's 1915 compilation of working class women's experiences of marriage and childbirth, *Maternity*. The sad reductionism of the potted biographies that complete each entry ("wages £1; 12 children, 1 stillbirth, 4 miscarriages"; "wages 14/- to £1; 3 children, 2 stillbirths, 2 miscarriages") reveal the depth of human suffering and relentless misery that passed as ordinary life less than a hundred years ago.

The popular women's magazines of the time (the sort Beth herself read when she could spare a copper or two to pay for them) are filled with advertisements for tonics purporting to offer cures for an array of illnesses symptomatic of depression. Dr Cassell's Tablets, for example, were advertised widely as being "Especially Suitable for Nursing Mothers and during the Critical Periods of Life", and were the recognised "Home Remedy for Nervous Breakdown, Nerve Paralysis, Infantile Paralysis, Neurasthenia, Sleeplessness, Anaemia, Kidney Trouble, Indigestion, Wasting Disease, Palpitation, Vital Exhaustion and Nervous Debility...."

Apart from advertisements for remedies, the popular press also carried letter and problem columns which contain numerous heartrending descriptions of the victims of what we would now call Chronic Fatigue Syndrome, bulimia and bipolar disease; glimpses of lives laid low by limited opportunities, poverty, endless struggle and constant pregnancy. The advice given to these exhausted, alienated and desperate women is in general kindly and homely in so far as it goes, and it must have been reassuring for at least some of the women reading it to know that they were not alone in their occasional quiet surrenders to stress and anxiety, but even so there is very little offered in the form of effective remedy. For the most part, the responsibility for their misery is placed firmly on the already over-burdened shoulders of the women themselves. They are routinely exhorted to "count their blessings", and to avoid "giving into gloominess".

More than one contemporary "weary wife" confided her secret dread that the baby she finds she is expecting will place an unsustainable strain on the family's already over-stretched resources, only to be told to cheer up and try doing her daily dozen in front of an open window. In these missives from the past, fresh air is frequently advocated as a solution to everything from grief to period pains and constipation.

Living at a time without washing-machines, contraceptives, discreet and hygienic sanitary protection and free health care, Beth and her contemporaries had every reason to feel stressed and anxious, but their misery was compounded by the deep fear, the social stigma, of anything to do with "nervous diseases" or "brain trouble". Suffering with your "nerves" may have been unavoidable and, according to the medical orthodoxy of the time, inevitable in women who were after all at the mercy of their bodies and menstrual cycles. But it was certainly not acceptable to talk too much about it. It was widely believed that not only was mental illness hereditary and an indication of bad blood, in nearly every case it had its origin in the dirty business of S-E-X.

The link between venereal syphilis and hereditary mental instability was well-known in the nineteenth century, but although that was stigmatic enough, it was not the only accepted cause. A standard medical work of 1918, *The Practitioner's Encyclopaedia of Midwifery and the Diseases of Women* (one of the most widely read of its type) confidently asserts the "modern scientific opinion" that a condition such as neurasthenia, for instance (very commonly diagnosed a century ago and often described in terms similar to modern-day Chronic Fatigue Syndrome), "has its origin in masturbation..." Elsewhere in the same work we are told that "anxiety neurosis" is caused by "repeated sexual excitation which is not allowed to obtain gratification", for example in the case of a married couple practising the withdrawal method of contraception. For women like Beth who dedicated themselves to the avoidance of shame and the pursuit of respectability with the same vigour they employed when scouring their doorsteps or outhouse seats, such "expert" opinion constituted a very sound reason why a woman should not blather on to all and sundry about the state of her nerves.

Add to this the terrible guilt, constantly reinforced in the women's journals, that each down and upswing in a mother's mood would adversely affect her children, especially her unborn children, it is indeed a wonder that more women of Beth's ilk did not find themselves locked in padded cells. An unborn child, as early twentieth-century women were repeatedly told in the standard guides to pregnancy and motherhood, needs to grow in the womb "surrounded by feelings of cheerful composure and love". No mother has the right to give herself up to "selfish worry" as it will almost certainly injure her child. An unborn baby's physical and mental disposition is so intimately connected to the mother, so sensitive to her mode of living and her state of mind, that anything which is injurious to her will be injurious to the foetus as well.

For this reason, pregnant women in the early twentieth century were told to avoid hard physical work, "too great a pressure of brain-work", and shocks and distress of any kind with the same gravity of tone employed by medical experts when warning against substances which could induce miscarriage. Many a wretched child, went the standard warnings, owes its feeble body and brain to its mother failing in her duty: they have been ruined by their mother's contact even before their birth. As the eugenics movement began to gather force in the pre-World War One era, it became the imperative of mothers to produce healthy children for the Empire. It was bad enough that some married women contemplated ridding themselves of potentially healthy children, but to wilfully inflict an idiot or crippled child upon the country might by some be considered a far worse offence.

And yet the extreme levels of stress endured by so many working-class women as they struggled to keep body and soul together in the early part of the last century could not fail to be heightened during pregnancy. When faced with the realisation that there was to be "still another baby with its inevitable consequences – more crowding, more illness, more worry, more work, and less food, less strength, less time to manage with…", in Maud Pember Reeves's words, only the most insensitive or stupid woman would have failed to give in to worry. Sometimes it was, as Beth would have said, enough to make you feel like giving in; but then what was the point, when just by thinking that way you only let yourself in for even more worry and guilt.

***

Beth gave birth to her second child, my grandfather's brother Stan, in the summer of 1907. She was, she later stated, quite happy to have left it so long; it is after all so much easier with just the one kiddie to take care of. When she fell again at first it was a shock, but then after a bit she found that she did not mind too much. It was not such a dreadful thing. Stan's birth came at a time of contentment. She had her little home, she adored her little Reggie and Bert was such a dear old thing. He might have had an easy-going (some might say a lazy) streak, and he really would-n't have noticed if the house was a pigsty, but all their life together he listened to her worries, was kind to her and did as she bid. If on occasion he could not prevent a puzzled expression from creeping across his brow as he tried to work out what she was on about, he more than made up for it by always being happy to do his bit.

During her pregnancy he was "maid of all work and bottle washer", as she liked to put it, a role he performed without a bit of complaining. Each day before he left for work at half past seven he would fetch in the water from the stand-by tap, and then move all of the furniture out of the way so she could run the broom or the mop across the floor. When he came in of an evening he helped her with the washing, doing all the dollying and wringing and lifting the coppers for her. They both knew that it was very important for her not to lift anything heavy: plenty brought on a slip that way, jumping up to throw wet sheets over the line, beating carpets, lifting the bath-tub, when they were far gone.

With such a helpful husband and only one little boy to look after, Beth had a bit more time to herself than she was used to. She spent it on reading her story papers. All her life she liked to read about the Royal Family, scandalous divorces and anything romantic and dreamy. She especially liked to read the descriptions of lovely wedding dresses in the society pages, "cream cashmere with lace trim and orange blossom tulle veil", "Parma violet silk trimmed with chiffon", "Dove coloured silk trimmed with canary net of Brussels lace fastened with orange blossom..." She liked to imagine the dresses and work out how she, a good needlewoman, might make them up, given half the chance. She later admitted that she had been quite selfish during her pregnancy, but she had no qualms about making the most of the luxury of time to herself. She knew that once the baby was there everything would be more difficult.

Bert's father died in 1910, an event which seems to have precipitated Bert's return to Romford, together with Beth and the two boys. Had Bert had enough of trudging off each day to the railway works? Was the lure of a potentially large cash settlement too good to refuse, even for Beth? Bert probably wanted to be close to his mother and siblings at such a time, but it is unlikely that he would have said as much to Beth. How did he persuade her to return to Romford? Perhaps she believed that her husband, the eldest son after all, would now come into his inheritance and the days of being looked down upon would end.

If so then she would have been very disappointed (though perhaps not entirely surprised) when it was discovered that the old man had left almost nothing to his eldest son. When his estate was settled, two years later, he was found to have left just £6/12/- (a sum equivalent to about £400 in today's money) out of the fortune he had amassed less than a decade before. The Woods always dealt in cash wherever possible, so it is difficult to say with any certainty whether this really was all that was left, and we may be sure that "what became of the rest of the money" was a matter of intense speculation for many years afterwards.

Over the years, Bert learnt to turn a deaf ear whenever Beth started on about how they had been "gypped" out of the fortune she was certain that her father-in-law had really left. Down through the years she would often threaten to return to Stony, but the fact was Bert had for once put his foot down. In the event, she did not go back there for years, not until her eldest son took her there for the odd day's outing in his motorcar.

Bert and Beth set up their new home in an old cottage (now gone – a print shop stands on the same spot today) on Como Road in the north of the town, close by the River Rom and Stickleback, or Tiddlebrat, Lane (as it would have been known to my grandfather and his little brother). This was a rickety wooden footbridge where the boys would have played their version of "pooh sticks" and fished for tiddlers. Cottons was still standing then, unoccupied, a short distance away, but Bert's younger brother was by now installed in Elm Lodge on the other side of Romford on the road out to Hare Street. He was enjoying a degree of success with his growing warehousing and removals business. My mother remembers Elm Lodge as a well-appointed house with a gravel drive where her great-uncle was still living at the time of his death in the early 1950s. In fact, it was not as grand as Cottons, being as its name suggests the small lodge house at the gateway to the Elms Estate, but it shows that there was a great disparity between the fortunes of the two brothers, and that Bert and Beth were definitely the "poor relations".

With the move back to Romford, Bert became an occasional employee in his brother's business, and gradually slipped back into his old higgling ways. The brothers were to step up the horse-trading once again at the start of World War One, but in the meantime they got by, developing a nice side line in "antique dealing", restoring and selling on anything that they picked up when doing the house removals. They also kept cows on some grazing land, which my uncle recalls was on the south side of Romford near the gravel pit. But these ploys apart Bert was evolving into that staple of small-town life in the last century: the genial bloke with a pony and trap, the early twentieth-century equivalent of a mini-cab driver. He worked just as hard as he needed to and the rest of the time hung about on "lazy corner" with the other local characters, popping into the Swan, or the Golden Lion up near the market.

Bert was content with his lot. He was easy-going to a fault and genuinely fond of his mother and brothers and sister; there was not one jealous bone in his body and far from being resentful of his brother's success, he actually liked working for him. But Beth hated being back in the Wood family's clutches and would have liked nothing more than to tell them all to take a running jump off a short plank. What was more, higgling and driving a dicky-cart about the place was hardly the respectable line she had imagined her future husband following. Disappointment must have layered on disappointment as she found that yet again she was in the position of trying to make ends meet, far removed from her own family, yet beholden to her in-laws – particularly when in February 1913, after a gap of six years, another child came along, a daughter this time, Kathleen May, or Maisie, as she came to be known.

Although she was always friendly to Bert's sister and the youngest brother, Beth nursed a bitter hatred towards Bert's mother and to a lesser extent his brother Alf. She abjured all offers of help and support from them, and all attempts at reconciliation were swiftly rebuffed. (Her hatred of them was so pervasive that years later, in the 1930s, when my grandfather needed some capital to help establish his millinery business, he refused to ask his uncle for help, even though he could have afforded it, much to the fury and incredulity of my grandmother. He knew that he could never have done so without incurring the wrath of his mother.) Beth only permitted Bert to take money from his brother if he had earned it, fair and square; and sides of bacon and Christmas turkeys sent from Elm Lodge were simply sent straight back.

What had they done to so inflame her? Had they really diddled Bert? Was he really such a fool that he failed to see it or had he preferred to turn a blind eye in the interest of harmonious family relations? Did he decide to do that even though it must have made life between Beth and him difficult on more than a few occasions? Or were the Woods right in their belief that Beth was, at least some of the time, "a difficult woman", "not all there". The reasons are lost to us; all that remains is the incandescent glow of that implacable fury.

***

My grandfather was twelve when World War One broke out in August 1914 and so he did not return to school the following September. To his (and his mother's) shame and regret, he went to work helping his dad and uncle with their renewed efforts to make some money out of the horses. This was a transitional period for him, put into long trousers and made to spend lonely days walking lines of mules down to Tilbury docks. It must have been at some time around this point that he had his wrist tattooed, a boy commemorating his newly acquired manhood.

According to family legend, Bert had wanted to sign up and do his bit, but although he was just thirty-four and in rude health the army rejected him, deciding that he was of far more value to the war effort staying put in Romford and supplying a steady stream of sturdy animals for the Front. Bert was very disappointed by the rejection, and, in the time of white feathers, yet another layer of shame wrapped itself around my grandfather's family. Bert is usually depicted as nothing more than a happy-go-lucky if somewhat dim-witted old cove (and his good nature would be sorely tested soon enough), but he was not immune to anxiety about what others made of him. When Beth drowned the twins and calamity descended upon his life, he told a reporter from the local paper that he was an ex-service-man, which was a plain lie. Perhaps he reasoned that he had indeed done his bit in providing the cavalry with hundreds and hundreds of well-trained horses for the Front.

The Great War did not give the horse trade the same boost as the Boer War had done, but there was enough of an upsurge in demand to keep the Wood brothers busy and happy. The army commandeered a hundred and sixty-five thousand steeds at the start of the war, and demand kept up as large numbers of the poor beasts came to grief in the thick mud of the battlefields. Eventually around fifteen thousand horses a month were being despatched to the Front, and by 1917 over half-a-million horses and quarter of a million mules were in use. Most of these were the "roughriders" of the type that Bert and his brother quickly trained up.

At the height of the trade, according to my grandfather, they were selling hundreds of horses each week to the army, a figure which I can hardly believe and have found hard to verify. However the demand was certainly there and the Woods knew the business better than most.

This period must have been a nerve-wracking time, to hear Zeppelins flying over Romford on their way to and from bombing raids in London and East Anglia. Many of those who lived in the south-east through both wars have said that it was the 1914-18 War which they remembered as being the worst one. It was after all the first time civilians had been under attack from strange flying machines and sudden and swift bombardments from the air. In one bombing raid over Essex, towards the end of the war, forty-seven people died.

In the middle of the war, July 1916, Beth gave birth to another boy, Alfie, after a gap of just three years, which was very short for her. She now had four children: Reg, aged 14, Stan, aged 9, Maisie, aged 3, and the new baby. The family had by then moved to a five-roomed terraced cottage (a typical three-up, two-down) on the London Road, not very far from Cottons. I have a photograph of some of their neighbours out in the backyard, and a large shed is visible where one of them kept a donkey and where Bert and Beth kept their tin bath. It is the same yard where Beth drowned the twins. This end of London Road, the end nearest the town, is now completely altered and the house long gone, but it probably stood close to a row of shops which included a pub, tea room, wheelwright and confectioners, and at least one seventeenth-century building. All of this stretch was cleared (along with Cottons) to make way for the ring road and the huge roundabout which today dominate the northern end of the town.

Beth was now living the sort of existence she had managed to avoid for the first ten years of her married life, with four children to look after, two of them under five. Bert might have been earning reasonably good money, but the stresses of daily life for a busy mother of four were compounded by the increasing difficulties of life during World

War One. German U-boats were destroying hundreds of thousands of tons of shipping bringing food and other supplies to Britain, and essentials such as potatoes and sugar were becoming very scarce. People had started to panic-buy and shops were under siege. It was, as Beth would have said, a great worry.

Then one day in March 1918 something happened which would change everything for Beth and Bert, forever. As usual, Beth spent much of the morning standing in the long queues that now stretched daily along Romford High Street, patiently waiting to collect her weekly rations: a quarter pound of butter and 1/3d worth of uncooked meat per person. As she stood waiting for her sausages in the line at Axon's, the butchers on the High Street, she might well have agreed with the lady in front of her that, yes, this war business gets one down. Things seemed in such a terrible muddle. Once outside with her parcel of meat tucked away carefully in her basket, she might have noticed the two soldiers in their putties standing by the kerbside as a motor car rattled past them, and they might have prompted her to wonder whether this awful business was going to end before her Reggie would be joining the next lot of troops marching out of Hare Hall camp. But she would have given them no more thought than that.

As she prepared to cross the road, Beth told Maisie to put her hands on the handle of the baby's pushchair and promised that if they were good she would buy them some chocolate at Muskett's up on South Street. Those two soldiers crossed with them and, as they passed by on the other side of the road, one of them sneezed in the direction of the little girl. Five days later Beth was facing the biggest crisis of her life.

***

It is time to introduce another family ghost. When my mother stayed at her Grandma Wood's cottage as a little girl in the 1940s she remembers a room filled with the relics of another little girl. Maisie's china dollies and hand-painted tea set have long since vanished, but my mother still has her tiny bone-handled knife, fork and spoon in their leather case lined with blue velvet. Like my mother before me, I used to love looking at the little cutlery set when I stayed with my grandparents, conjuring up a picture of sweet little Maisie, the only and adored girl in a family of big strapping boys. I was, I confess, more than a little jealous of her. I yearned for a big brother and adored my grandfather who had loved her so much, and I never owned anything as lovely as the little leather case with its pretty contents. There are no photographs of Maisie: the cutlery set is all that remains of this lost child.

The symptoms of diphtheria generally appear within five days of initial infection, which is usually through droplets spread by close contact with someone who is incubating or already suffering from the illness. At first there is little indication of the severity of the illness to come. The child will complain about her head hurting and then that her throat is a bit sore when she tries to swallow. The mother pressing her lips to the forehead will detect a slight fever, but at first will try and allay the instinctive concern she might be feeling. She will tuck the little one up in bed, maybe giving her a picture book to look at, all the while worrying that the eyes look brighter and glassier than usual. Soon the glands in the child's neck will begin to swell as the lining of the throat becomes coated in an exudate, a pale grey or white membrane teeming with the bacterium C. diphtheiae, which thickens until the child begins to experience severe difficulty in breathing. Her distressing struggle for breath produces nothing but a croupy gasp, which nonetheless resounds throughout the house. Her temperature climbs higher until delirium sets in, the pulse beats faster and the little one goes into shock. Fighting the panic clutching her heart, the mother knows that the doctor must be sent for.

One of the most dreadful sights for inhabitants of the little village of Dagenham at the turn of the last century was that of the black single horse-carriage galloping past with a nurse clutching a red blanket on board. This was the ambulance summoned from Rush Green Isolation Hospital to some stricken household in the surrounding area. Locals seeing it hurtle past would stop and say a little prayer, hoping that whoever it had gone to fetch would be going home again within a little while. While the ambulance waited outside the house on London Road, the nurse wrapped

Maisie in the red blanket and the cab driver carried her down the stairs. Bert and Beth were left standing in the street watching helplessly as the black cab drove away with their daughter on board on the 16th March, 1918. Later that day the council-men came and fumigated the house. Most of Maisie's clothes, toys and books were burnt in the bonfire they set in the backyard, only the china tea-set, a couple of dollies and the little knife and fork set survived. The whole family were tested for signs of infection: there was particular anxiety for the baby, Alfie, but fortunately the boys were all fine. Beth kept her house spic and span, and although the three boys all shared a room, Maisie had her own and so the infection had been well contained.

By the time Maisie reached the isolation hospital she was almost completely paralysed by the toxin which was now spreading throughout her central nervous system, attacking her heart and other vital organs. A tracheotomy was performed, making an incision in the child's throat to expose the trachea to the air, bypassing the thickened membrane. A little straw was stuck into the pulsating wound as the small child gasped and struggled for breath. It was, the doctors said, touch and go. Every day for a week Bert drove Beth in the trap to Dagenham, where they would enquire politely at the hospital gates after the health of their little girl. They were never allowed in to see her. Even when children had survived the danger point of their illness and were convalescing, their parents were only permitted to look at them for a few minutes each day through the thick glass windows of the hospital ward. After receiving the dreadful news that Maisie was no better, Bert and Beth had nothing else to do but return home. They sat in silence in the kitchen, trying to gather the strength required to go through the motions for the sake of the other children. How they must have wished that there was something more that they could do: soothe, comfort, cuddle her, or even just see for themselves how bad it went with Maisie.

They filled up the moments in between the ebb and flow of fear and hope by trying to think about something, anything, else. They lay awake, only occasionally drifting into sleep before waking suddenly with the feeling they had forgotten something, then sinking under the weight of remembrance. They made fervent prayers, pledged their hearts and souls, hoped against hope that the events of the past days would turn out to be nothing more than a nightmare. Worse of all, they imagined that they could hear Maisie skipping in the passageway or crying for them. They were struck by how silent and empty the house seemed without her. As soon as they could the next morning they would set off again in silence down the road to Rush Green.

A day or so towards the end the little girl slipped into a coma, no longer knowing if her mummy was there or not, stroking her damp curls, holding her hand, willing her to come home again. That morning when Beth went as usual to the gates she was told that the matron wanted to see her.

"I'm afraid that your little girl is very ill," she was told. "You can come into the room, but you must keep your distance from the cot. If she sees you and tries to cry, that will finish her." Bert and Beth stood side by side in the doorway looking down at their sleeping child, hardly daring to breathe in case they disturbed her: she looked so peaceful. After a while the nurse motioned to them that it was time to leave. There was nothing more anyone could do. The only sure remedy for diphtheria is a dose of antibiotics, not available to poor little Maisie in March 1918. Even today the disease (mercifully rare, thanks to routine innoculation) can be fatal for a large proportion of sufferers.

Maisie was only a little thing and her tiny white coffin fitted under the driver's box seat in the glass-sided hearse. This saved Bert a few bob, but he still had to find 1/3d for the death certificate, 2/- for the grave-diggers, another two bob for the hearse attendants and a half-a-crown for the laying-out women, a tanner (6d) for some flowers and a bob each for black ties for himself, Reg and Stan. Still, it was important to give your child a proper send off. He walked as proudly as he could manage behind the carriage with his two eldest sons either side of him.

It took half an hour for the cortège to pass along London Road and down St Andrew's Road, past the church where he and Beth had been married nearly seventeen years before, under the railway bridge on to Waterloo Road, turning right at Oldchurch Road and passing the workhouse before arriving at the gates of the cemetery. As they passed men lifted their hats as a mark of respect to the little procession, and women told their children to be quiet and bow their heads as they silently thanked the Lord that it was not one of theirs.

The little coffin was laid to rest in Crow Lane cemetery in a plot paid for by Bert's parents – his dad's final resting place was just a short distance away. All of Bert's family were waiting at the grave-side, old Mrs Wood, his brothers and sister and all their spouses. Beth stayed at home with little Alfie – the heavy curtains drawn against the light in every window in the little house, a piece of cloth wrapped around the doorknocker – sitting in the eerie silence. Hush now, Maisie's gone to Heaven. Don't cry. Don't cry.

***

The penny a week Bert and Beth had paid into the Burial Insurance Club for each of their children since birth would have barely covered the cost of Maisie's funeral, yet keeping up the payments on the Burial Insurance was an absolute priority in my grandfather's family, and many others like it. Some working-class children even went without new boots and extra food in order to make provision for their own funerals, and thus avoid the final indignity of a pauper's grave. But the insurances, like most of the other schemes poor families paid into, the Divi, the Boot, Stocking, Christmas and Crockery clubs, in a desperate attempt to make the pennies go a bit further, were a dreadful scam. The sale of funeral insurances to the working class was also big business, netting millions every year for companies such as the "Pru" and "Pearl Life Assurance". "No living child", wrote Maud Pember Reeves in 1913, "is better fed or better clothed because its parents, decent folk, scraped up a penny a week to pay the insurance collector on its account."

My grandfather kept up the insurance Bert and Beth took out for him with the Pru all his life, through thick and thin, just as his parents had told him do. He believed that this precaution would assure him a proper send-off without incurring needless financial worry for his relatives. When he died aged nearly eighty the cash value of the policy was just three hundred pounds, at a time when even a simple funeral cost almost twice that.

So scarred was my grandfather by the death of his little sister that when my mother took ill with scarlet fever at the age of four, twenty-five years later, he was literally paralysed by the shock. Unable to keep himself upright he fell against the staircase in the hallway, moaning incoherently. My grandmother – pretty upset herself – had to deal with the doctor and the journey to the isolation hospital alone.

For six weeks my mother languished in the children's ward unable to receive any visitors. Once better, her boredom and loneliness was only relieved by the gifts of comics and sweets my grandmother left at the gate for her, but even this simple gesture was beyond my grandfather: it would have required confronting deep dark fears and he found it easier to remove himself and remain tight-lipped and hollow-cheeked.

What were the scenes brought back to his mind? Did his mum and dad, for the most part quiet and controlled, give in to wild scenes of despair and grief? Did they sit and rock themselves to and fro, moaning like the wind down the chimney? Or was it the mute dignified carriage of the utterly desolate that affected him so much as a teenager? Oh, if it were my child, please God forbid, I would scream and wail and howl like an animal, tear the hair from my head, throw myself on the ground and roll in the dirt. I feel sure about this because I have played out the scene so many times (which mother has not?) every time one son is a few minutes late home from school or another runs on ahead of me and disappears out of sight around a corner. There have been nights when I have lain there overwhelmed with the burden of all that worry and asking myself how can I possibly sustain it? How can I hold my nerve, how can I find the courage to trust the wider world, the future: all the spaces where my children will go without me? I have lost count of the number of times I have promised my soul to whatever is lurking there in the shadows that edge my life, if only they can assure me that I will be mouldy in my grave long, long before my sons are laid in theirs.

It is easy to console ourselves with the thought that maybe once the worst that can possibly happen has happened to a person relief ensues, and there is respite from the worry that bedevils parents, that gnaws at our bones, our hearts and our souls. But really that is nonsense. If it is sometimes hard to imagine waking up yet again to carry on with the job of worrying and fearing for one's children, how much harder must it be to wake up and carry on with yet another day of loss and grief? To see the empty place at the dinner table, the little shoes lined up against the wall, the dust gathering on the little tea set. How could anyone bear it? Poor Beth, how ever did she find the strength to carry on attending to the needs of her boys, the youngest one just two years old?

Well, as Beth would have said with a little shrug, you just have to, don't you, dear? But it broke her heart, and in the end it sent her stark raving mad.

-11-

"A healthy infancy is a natural prelude to a vigorous youth and manhood and a capacity for doing a full share of the world's work."

Hugh T Ashby, author of *Infant Mortality*, 1915

It must have been hard for Beth, so soon after losing Maisie, to see my grandfather, as soon as he turned sixteen in April 1918, go off to the drill hall to collect his uniform. Keen to do his bit, he volunteered to join the 4th Battalion of the Essex Regiment, the Territorials. Plenty of boys of sixteen, and a good few who were even younger volunteered for the regular army, and found themselves at the Front (the legal age of conscription was eighteen in 1918), but Reg had promised his mum he would not do that. The shock would kill her, she said. All the same, he enjoyed his time in the Territorials, staying with them long after the war ended. Always a keen amateur photographer, he has left behind a clutch of photographs suffused with affection. These snaps record happy times spent with his army pals in camp at nearby St. Osyths and Jaywick Sands, the battalion football team, and the military band in which he played clarinet until he was well into his twenties. No doubt the army gave him a welcome opportunity to escape the terrible aura of repressed, muted sadness at home.

In the last year of the war there were over four million British men fighting, and every day the newspapers were full of incitements to the courage of the nation's motherswhose duty it was to bear, to rear and then to lose. By the end of the war it was officially reckoned that three-quarters of a million sons would not be coming home again. Right up until the final stages, the war machine sought out more and more men to gobble up. In April 1918 (when my grandfather took himself along to volunteer) the age limit for conscripts was raised to fifty and some of the exemptions which had hitherto kept younger men out of uniform were dropped.

Beth was lucky that none of her men were sacrificed on a Flanders' field, but she had not been spared sacrifice. She was a victim of another war, one being waged closer to home. Between 1911 and 1915, fifty per cent of all children aged between five and nine years died of infectious diseases in England and Wales. During the years of World War One sixty-three per cent of non-war related deaths were classified as "premature". And, as the war reached its climax, Beth was descending into a private hell.

A mother who loses a child blames nobody so much as she blames herself. For a year following Maisie's death Beth felt compelled to tell everyone she met that her daughter had died because a soldier had sneezed on the child. She felt it was her duty to warn others of the terrible threat that lurked everywhere, to let them know how easy it was to lose a child. She would often break down, crying bitterly, overwhelmed with her own helplessness, with the futility of all her efforts to protect and take care. She had long since, months ago, given up worrying about crying in front of other people: it was, she said, about the only thing she didn't worry about any more. She had finally become inured to the embarrassment of others, and she no longer noticed them look away or heard them when they tried to reassure her: "There, there. Don't take on so, dear." She barely felt the comforting pats on her arm. But what others thought of you did matter, and it would not be long before Beth would find herself dependent upon, at the mercy of, the opinions of others.

Beth was not the only person for whom the final months of the war slipped by in a daze of grief, as the tally of anxieties mounted up. In May 1918, barely two months after Maisie's death, the first British victim of the influenza pandemic died in Glasgow. Within a few weeks the virus had spread throughout the entire country; by October people were dropping like flies from influenza and the streets were being sprayed with disinfectant. By the end of the year influenza had claimed the lives of two hundred and twenty eight thousand people: the highest mortality rate for any illness in Britain since the cholera epidemics of the 1840s.

The soldiers who had survived the unsanitary conditions of the trenches were its chief agents. By the time the virus died out a year later, more than forty million people were dead worldwide: fourteen million more than the contemporary estimates of war dead.

As if this was not enough to contend with, there were terrifying rumours that everyone was being slowly poisoned by mustard gas, or some devilish variation concocted by the Kaiser. By the time the Armistice came to be signed, at five o'clock in the morning of November 11th 1918, the nation was bracing itself for an uncertain future. Prices were creeping up as basic foods became more and more scarce. And the insane asylums were full of young men, lately returned from the Front, unable to do anything but sit staring into space: a new term, "shellshock", fell into common usage.

As far as Bert was concerned, now that the army would no longer be taking orders of hundreds of horses each week from him and his brother, he was facing a serious drop in income and had no choice but to go back to helping his brother in the removals business. They would eventually become quite skilled at spotting and selling on anything of value that turned up in the course of the day, unwanted deceased effects – that sort of thing – but he knew that he and Beth were looking at a lean time all the same. Bert never allowed himself to think too deeply and gloomily about things, but he was as worried as the next man about the future, still grieving the loss of his little girl, and very concerned about Beth.

Christmas that year was bad, the worst any of them had ever known. Beth just could not seem to bring herself together; she found everything such an effort. Bert was used to Beth being strong and capable. In all the years (more than twenty) that he had known her, he had never seen her so down. He was so worried about her that he did something which if she had known about it would have been sure to make her wild: he confided in his mother. The old lady told Bert that in her opinion the best thing would be for him to give Beth another little one to "fill the gap" left by their precious Maisie. By February 1919, Beth, aged 41, was pregnant for the fifth and final time. A few weeks later, when she knew for sure, she told Bert that the news was "a bit of hope" for the future.

***

The Great War might have officially ended in November 1918, but Apocalypse was there on the horizon, with Famine and Pestilence following hard on the heels of War and Death. The tanks recently returned from the Western Front were soon to be found on the streets of Liverpool, where massed troops fixed bayonets and fired volleys over the heads of thousands of strikers and rioters. The Russian civil war was still being fought, and thousands of British soldiers were to be enjoined in the struggle until September 1919. The call for recruits to fight against Bolshevism was met by many of those who had returned from France, only to find that they were now unemployed and on the breadline, and so had little choice but to go back into uniform again. Others had returned from the trenches with a quite different political agenda, and were among the ninety thousand thronging Glasgow's George Square when the Red Flag was hoisted on a lamppost at the end of January 1919.

The Riot Act had to be read. In the period immediately following World War One, Britain was closer to social revolution than at any other time in the twentieth century. Workers in every area of trade and industry were rising up, demanding fixed working hours and minimum wages. A coal strike was followed by railway strikes, then workers in the ship and dockyards of London, Clydeside, Manchester and Belfast all downed their tools. Before it was out, the year 1919 would lose thirty-five million working days through strike action. Even the Metropolitan Police joined the clamouring discontentment, and the harsh treatment the striking officers received from the government prompted a further wave of sympathy strikes.

The strikes were in large part prompted by concerns about the mass unemployment which now threatened every area of industry in the country. Each day fifty thousand men were demobbed, many of them shell-shocked, blind, limbless. They poured into the towns and cities looking for work that did not exist, and by March 1919 over a million men were drawing the "out of work donation". Many of them took to roaming the countryside, drifting into petty crime and worse. The newspapers were filled with shocking reports of homeless, jobless, confused, hungry and damaged young people, caught "having relations" with one another in barns and ditches, stealing, begging and prostituting themselves. Many of them were identified as "war heroes" "formerly of good character", and coming from "respectable homes".

How my great-grandparents must have shuddered when they read about such "goings-on" in the *News of the World*. Beth probably tried to put it all out of her mind, thinking about the baby growing inside her, but of course it "got you down". She began to wonder if she was right to bring a baby into "such an awful world". A pregnant woman's connection to the wider world feels more vital, somehow, than at any other time in her life. Her senses propelled through a seemingly more vivid space than the one the rest of humanity inhabits: she is alert, ultra-sensitive to everything around her. As her pregnancy began to advance, Beth, still overladen with grief at losing Maisie, began to feel as if there was nothing to her but worry. Her head, she would later explain, "felt enormous", and however hard she tried she could not escape the anxiety that she had no idea how they would all "manage to carry on".

Sometimes, she said, she felt as if she was stuck on "an island of her own misery", miles and miles from anyone else. She had dreams about trying to sail to the island of happiness she could see "over there" on the horizon. She wondered whether the sadness would ever leave her, and then she felt guilty for thinking that way knowing that she could never let herself forget about Maisie. When she tried to look into the future all she could see was "a shadow over everything". She began to worry that this meant that she was going to die, that she would not be able to "stop" herself from leaving Bert alone to cope with the boys and the new baby. She was crying every day, and she was worried about the effect that was having on the new baby and also on little Alfie, "the poor little mite", who was "miserable and grizzling all the while". She knew it was wrong of her to give in to these feelings, but she just didn't seem to be able to bring herself round.

Meanwhile daily life was becoming even more of a strain than it had been during the war. Bert and Reg were earning, but for how long? There were no guarantees, the way things were going. The middle boy, Stan, now aged twelve, would be out of school in another year, and, hopefully, earning along with his dad and his older brother, but Beth fretted that he might not be able to find an occasion. (She was still worrying about Stan's ability to earn a living twenty years later, during the Second World War). There were so many men unable to find work; thousands were looking at ruin. What if they were among them?

Gas, electricity, sugar and meat were still all on ration. The bakers were on strike and many homes were running out of bread. Beth always baked her own, but there was a severe shortage of flour and before long the government would impose a ban on fancy cakes and pastries in an attempt to preserve dwindling stocks. In Ilford, just a few miles down the London Road from Romford, women fainted as they queued for bread in the extreme heat of the summer of 1919.

Elsewhere, so many others were starving that plenty of people believed they would be next. A war widow and her children (one a teenaged boy lately returned from the Front) were found living in a cowshed in East Anglia, subsisting on a diet of hedgerow fruit and stolen eggs. In Pembrokeshire another war widow (and mother of six) starved herself to death in order to feed her children, after a bureaucratic bungle prevented her from receiving her army separation allowance for seven weeks.

But Beth's great dread was that she would lose another one of hers through disease. She was still warning everyone she stopped to talk to when she did her shopping, and clutching Alfie to her whenever they came into contact with strangers. She hated Reg going to the Drill Hall: she knew that a lot of the fellows he was mixing with there had only very lately returned from the trenches, and was sure that they were spreading all sorts of germs and illnesses. The last case in the Spanish flu pandemic had occurred, we now know, in May 1919, but the newspapers remained jittery with stories of possible further outbreaks for the rest of the year, and the health authorities continued to urge vigilance, and the avoidance of close contact with anyone coughing and sneezing. The heavily pregnant Beth took the warnings more seriously than did most. Her fear was heightened when she read in the paper that there had been an outbreak of plague in London.

Beth's days were long, beginning at six or seven in the morning, when she finally gave up trying to sleep and went downstairs to fix the breakfast for Bert and the boys, and to light the fire for the copper. The copper was built into the corner of the gloomy little scullery, and was kept on the boil all day, giving rise to great clouds of steam. With the kettle hissing, and its lid clattering on top of the range, the linens draped about it to dry, pots of stew or broth, and great fat puddings bubbling away, the tiny scullery was like a Turkish bath by mid-morning, and quite unbearable in the heat of the day. Yet Beth was loath to move herself or Alfie too far away from it. While the little one played with some empty cotton reels or left-over dough, she would sweep and mop down the kitchen, the stairs and the passage, clean out the grate, scrub the front step. Before long it was dinner-time and Bert and Reg would be home from work and Stan from school, all looking for their grub. For them life was returning to normality. She really did not blame them, but she could not help but wonder what would have happened if they had never come back to Romford.

Beth, a marvellous cook who was stick-thin her whole life, did not often eat much. When she did have a bit of time to herself she might take a cup of tea with a slice of bread and marge, while she tried to read one of her "books". During her last pregnancy she skipped meals, and was painfully thin by the time she came to be delivered. When Bert tried to coax her into sitting and eating with them, she told him she didn't feel hungry in the heat. She told others that she was trying to scrape together the twelve bob she needed for Mrs Bennett, the midwife, and the five shillings she had promised to her friend, Mrs Moss, who was going to come and stay for the first fortnight to help with the housework and the new baby. But Bert was earning a reasonable amount, and so was Reg, and there was no real need for Beth to starve herself for such necessities. Bert's mother told him that he should keep an eye on Beth, that in her opinion she was going barmy, and it would all go badly for her when she came to have the baby. He told her to keep her opinions to herself, one of the only times in his life he had ever dared contradict his mother. All the same Bert worried.

Beth spent a great deal of her time sewing, the only thing that calmed her nerves and took her mind off her worries. There were always collars and cuffs to be turned, and heaps of darning, even though she always knitted double heels (because boys are so hard on their socks). She was working hard on the layette for the baby, adding to the growing pile of little flannel nightgowns, Turkey towelling night bibs, lawn cotton day-gowns, white bengaline bonnets. Her sewing was better than her knitting, but even so she made half-a-dozen little woollen vests, a wool jacket, a wrapping shawl and two pairs of bootees. Beth had no idea that she was expecting triplets, and she was so small that, looking at her, nobody else would have thought it for a moment, so she had no idea that she should have been producing at least double the number of little items.

It required a terrific effort on her part, but she had noticed that her nerves were worse than ever if she stayed cooped up inside all day. So she did her best to get out at least once. This meant lying on the bed to wrap the maternity belt around her girth. The maternity belt was required wearing for all expectant mothers up until the 1930s. It consisted of two-and-a-half yards of strong huckaback towelling, folded into a four-inch thickness, and pulled tight over the hips and around the waist. There were two long thick strips of webbing sewn onto the back of the towelling which, with some effort, the woman stretched over her shoulders before pinning them in place at the front of the towelling band, so that her breasts were pushed flat. Two sets of thick pink rubber suspenders were attached to the lower edge of the towelling belt to keep up the thick black stockings, which were worn whatever the weather. It was a struggle for a pregnant woman to pull them on, sitting on the edge of the bed, and reaching, with difficulty, over her bump in order to stretch them over her feet and roll them up her legs. Once the belt and stockings were on a woman would cover herself up with long-sleeved flannel combinations, a knitted corset and a white underskirt. Then the dark skirt, seersucker blouse and, in spite of the heat, a sacque jacket, long and loose enough to conceal her figure out of doors. Now was not the time to be seen in public in anything too tight or too revealing or too gaudy, or anything, in short, which might draw attention to her condition. Finally she pinned her hat in place: it would never do to be seen out of doors without a hat on.

Going out helped Beth to take her mind off things, and that was important for the new baby's wellbeing. She liked to look at the table damasks in Stones up on Market Place, and carefully inspect fish and meat and vegetables, checking the hue, holding each item up to sniff and weigh it in her hands before buying, like Mrs Gibberd had taught her to do when she was in service. On Wednesdays she would try and take a turn about the market looking for bargains – remnants of cloth, nice pieces of china, skeins of cheap wool. Even in the heat, a walk was a sure way to ease the back pains, stop the varicose veins and keep everything flowing. People sometimes asked her how she was managing, and she always replied that she held her condition to be a blessing after her sad loss. And then she would find herself crying yet again.

Back home in the evening, with the tea things out of the way and the younger boys off to bed, she might try and put her feet up and do a bit more sewing or knitting, while Bert sat smoking his pipe and reading the *Sketch*. He never asked her how she was feeling, but he did notice. He would put his arm about her whenever he saw her beginning to slump. He tried to keep his own emotions hidden from her, preferring to take them down the pub for a spell each evening, and nurse them along with a pint of ale. But Beth saw him as he sat in the kitchen of a night with his paper spread out on the table in front of him. It looked as if he was squinting against the cloud of pipe smoke as he tried to read, but she could tell that he was struggling to hold back tears that threatened to stream down his dear, weather-beaten, old face.

If there was enough oil in the lamp, she might settle down with a mug of cocoa and a little bit of bread and cheese or a nice biscuit, but she often found it hard to swallow. She would flick through one of her "books", but it was hard to concentrate and follow the stories. "Tell the Mystery Woman your dreams. She will enlighten you. Tell her your troubles. She will help you. Tell her your problems. She will advise you"; "Is Love at First Sight Possible?"; "Read the New Story of a Girl who Placed Riches First".

By nine, she would be upstairs trying to sleep, with Bert's large, already snoring form lying beside her. Staring up at the shadows on the ceiling she would tell herself that it was important to sleep, that the baby would be nervy, that she should just try and drift off. It was strange, but even though she was so weary that her poor old bones ached, she just couldn't put her mind to rest. All day long, her head feeling a tremendous size, with the queer sensation that she were floating away, she longed to lie down. But as soon as she climbed into bed all the hopelessness and worry came out of the blackness and fell upon her.

What if things went bad for her in the confinement and she wasn't able to do her housework and the children weren't kept clean and took ill? What if something went wrong? How ever would Bert manage without her? What if he gave up and chucked it all in? What would happen to the children? She was thinking that even after her death the worry would still be there, tormenting her, twisting her thoughts this way and that. She was thinking that there was never going to be any escape: that she was now and forever a great mass of worry. Oh, she often wondered how it was she had come to this, when all she had ever done was just try to get on, when she had always been so steady? She found herself thinking of her poor old mum more and more. She saw herself growing old and weary, and had an awful feeling that her life was somehow all used up. When she looked in the mirror it was Lou she saw there, looking back at her: Lou to the life.

Finally, just before she drifted into the sleep of late pregnancy, jagged with hallucinations and sensation, she asked what it was that she would have to give in return for the guarantee that she would never again have to bury any more of her children. What would it take: an arm, eye teeth, her life, her soul? What do you offer when you make your secret pledges to God or the Devil or Yahweh or Allah or whoever it is you pray to in those endless hours when the sheets stick to you and the shadows gather all around, as you lie awake waiting for the next little cough from the room next door?

***

On the July 2nd 1919, as Beth prepared to enter her final month of pregnancy, the formal Proclamation of Peace was read from the balcony of St James's Palace, and then taken in procession to Charing Cross, Temple Bar and Wood Street, where, on the steps of the Royal Exchange, it was read again. Fanfares sounded, the air rung with the cheers of the gathered crowds, and the skies temporarily darkened as a great cloud of hats was flung up.

On July 19th there were official peace celebrations throughout the land, including at Romford. My grandfather turned out for the military band, and his dad and two little brothers went down to watch him, splendid in his uniform, play his clarinet. A few days later, in stark contrast to the earlier jubilation, the streets of London were stone silent when fitey thousand survivors of the War to End all Wars marched on Hyde Park, in memory of their 743,702 "fallen" comrades. The long grave column of broken men and grieving widows and children, tears shining in their eyes, moved slowly past like spectres, without uttering a sound.

On August 6th, Parliament offered a vote of thanks to all those mothers who had produced strong sons for the Front. The *News of the World* gave away more than sixty thousand blue and white tin trays, a token of a grateful nation's esteem, to all mothers of ten children or more who applied for one. It was a small consolation at a time when, for most people, life was short on hope. Estimates for the Retail Price Index show that it had more than doubled since 1916 (the biggest jump since the eighteenth century), yet wages for the working man, that is those not already among the growing hordes of unemployed, were still scarcely more than their 1914 level.

The lion share of the worry and striving fell to the women, and there were many who found themselves simply unable to cope. A thirty-seven-year-old miner's wife was found with her throat cut in the family's outhouse. In the note she left she told her husband, "I'm tired of my life. I have been a failure and have been wasting too much money."

On August 19th, getting up before daylight, the wife of an unemployed grocer's assistant in Fawkham, Kent, and mother of seven, told her husband that she was going for a drink of water. Later he found her in the garden near to the water tank wherein lay the body of their thirteen-month-old son. A few days later two newly born babies were found wrapped in brown paper in the bushes at Liverpool's Sefton Park. They had been strangled with bootlaces. In Ilford a policeman apprehended a woman carrying a dead baby through the streets. When challenged, the woman said that she had been unable to give the baby any milk because her husband was out of work. On inspection it was found that the baby had indeed died from starvation. Both parents were found guilty of manslaughter.

***

The last week of Beth's confinement, in mid-August 1919, the weather was very hot: the temperature in the shade reached 91°F (33°C). The medical officer's notices, warning mothers about the summer diarrhoea, had been up in the town centre for almost a month and Beth had read every line of them until she knew them by heart. The phrase "keep the premises free from any accumulation of filth" in particular preyed on her mind. She was keeping both the front and back doors open, but the warm, still current of air passing through the little three-up two-down didn't seem to her to be doing much good; just encouraging the flies to come in. The blessed pests hung in clusters in the gloomy passage and in the little kitchen, deftly avoiding the flypapers she had hung there, chasing each other around in circles until she felt dizzy looking at them.

During the day she had been opening the window in the boys' room (she really could not bear to go into Maisie's room) to let in the fresh air, but one of them kept closing it at night. Then again, when the window was open, she found herself climbing the stairs all the while to check that the flies weren't coming in there. The effort and the worry made her sick and light-headed, and yet if she left the window closed she worried that there was not enough fresh air, and the boys needed fresh air in the room. "Overcrowding is a cause of Diarrhoea", was another of the Medical

Officer's phrases she incessantly turned over in her mind.

She was also obsessively checking beneath the little lace cover she kept over the milk jug. She had stitched a row of little blue beads around the edge of it to weigh it down and keep it in place, but even so she was still worried that the flies were somehow slipping in underneath it, and laying their eggs in the milk. Perhaps the milk was already contaminated. She wondered how she could tell for sure. Many times a day she considered throwing the whole lot away. She started to boil the milk before giving it to anyone in their tea, and she took to giving Alfie watered down Nestlé's in his dish of tea, throwing away any that was left in the tin. It was dear, and she worried about the expense and the waste, but she really was so afraid of taking any risks. She was washing up, mopping floors, sweeping and dusting until the sweat ran down her; she was using twice as much soap as usual; she was scrubbing out the privy every day until the wooden seat was chalky white; and she had been on and on at Bert to lime-wash the walls.

But in her heart she knew that all her efforts were futile. There was nothing she could do if a fly decided to come in and lay its eggs in her milk jug. Her life was now a continuing battle with dirt which she knew she could never be sure of winning. There was always the filth that she couldn't even see, the filth that had nothing to do with her, and about which she could do nothing.

And the heat had really brought out the smells from the other yards. They kept the donkey mucked out, in the back, but the heat made it bad again as soon as it was done. There were great black clouds of flies hovering over the pavings outside the front door, and so she was keeping Alfie indoors with her, however much he grizzled with boredom. She felt better that way, even with him under her feet. At least there she could keep an eye on him.

**

Beth went into labour late on the night of Saturday 16th August. She was just thirty-three weeks into the pregnancy, a little premature. Bert was worried, but he had been expecting something to happen for a while. Beth had let herself grow very thin, and she was worrying herself to death about everything, even though he kept telling her not to fret. Typically, she had started to make everything ready as soon as she felt the first twinges. She had not been able to afford a mackintosh to protect the mattress, and the cheaper American cloth was difficult to come by so soon after the war and the cotton strikes, so she began by putting down a yard-square piece of brown paper, padded out with several sheets of newspaper, which she had sewn together a few days before. She had also made up some draw-sheets out of old linen and placed one of these over the mattress as well.

She later told her friend, Mrs Moss, that she was glad she had thought of doing all this in good time and not been caught by surprise. She thought that, perhaps, she had had some inkling that it was all going to start sooner rather than later. She had also thought to cut up some sanitary napkins for herself with the left-over scraps of linen, and was boiling them up, prior to drying them in the oven, when her friend Mrs Moss arrived to help.

Bert showed Mrs Moss into Maisie's room, which nobody had used for more than a year. Once she was settled in there, Mrs Moss helped Beth to prepare the lying-in room for the midwife. The two women swept down the walls, scrubbed the floor and wiped the bedstead with a rag soaked in turps. When this was done Beth took a dose of castor-oil and put out the baby clothes to air. Then she had a good wash, and boiled up some water in a clean, scalded jug which she placed on the nightstand with a clean cloth over it. Mrs Moss made up another kettle and placed it, along with the hand basins, the tin bath, some vinegar, a tot or two of brandy, a clean flannel sheet, some lengths of strong wax threads, a pair of scissors, some sterilised wool, a piece of soft linen to wipe the baby's eyes, a bar of soap and a nailbrush, on a scrubbed deal table. Everything was now ready for Mrs Bennett.

With all the preparations done, there was nothing for Beth to do but potter about the house until she felt ready to lie on the bed. She spent the time knitting, chatting to Mrs Moss and waiting for nature to take its course. Mrs Moss later reported that Beth was very talkative and seemed to be as well as could be expected, although she was a little apprehensive about the baby coming before its time, and every now and again she would cry whenever Maisie's name came up in the conversation. Still, she was up to joking with Mrs Moss, saying that she was looking forward to the luxury of spending nine days in bed, the number of days newly delivered mothers were expected to rest for at the time.

It was Mrs Bennett, the midwife, not Dr Jeaffreson, who attended Beth at the birth. Beth had decided that the guinea for the doctor was an unnecessary expense. She was not a young, first-time mother: she was forty one years old and had already produced three strapping sons, as well as her sweet little girl, Maisie. If she had known that she was expecting triplets she might have reconsidered, but she had absolutely no idea. Multiple births were a rarity in the past: twins occurred less than once every ten thousand births or so, and triplets were virtually unheard of, a veritable freak of nature. Maud Pember Reeves reported that a favourite entertainment of many working-class couples was reading about multiple births in the newspapers. Bert and Beth might have done so themselves on occasion, no doubt thankful that they were not the poor couple in question.

Mrs Bennett, the midwife, arrived at about one in the morning, when Beth had been in the early stages of labour for several hours, and she would have wasted no time in administering a soap and water enema, before shaving and bathing Beth's privates with a solution of lysol. The birth was very difficult. The waters had broken in a gush in the wake of a violent shuddering pain, and Beth laboured right through the night, until the first fingers of light were reaching through the heavy curtains at the bedroom window. Mrs Bennett had put her onto her side, instructing her to pull on the roller-towel fixed to the end of the bed and to bear down. She later recalled that Beth was very good, and hardly made a fuss at all, although it was very hard on her and the old midwife had felt quite sorry for the poor lady.

Beth afterwards reported that all through her ordeal Mrs Bennett and Mrs Moss were kindness itself; she was ever so glad to have had them both there. The two women took turns to press down against the small of Beth's back, and reminded her to keep her eyes closed to avoid straining her eyeballs. Occasionally Mrs Moss would give Beth a little sip of beef tea to keep up her strength, and when Beth started to flag she gave her a little nip of the brandy on a spoon. Towards the end Mrs Bennett gave her some sugar water to help the uterine muscles expel the baby, and rubbed her perineum with a little Vaseline.

The first baby, a lovely little girl, came through quite quickly. But Mrs Bennett could see that there was a second baby, also a girl, tucked up behind, and that the little thing was breech. Mrs Bennett applied pressure to Beth's abdomen until she could feel that the tiny legs were in the correct position. Beth could feel the midwife's finger inside her pushing up along the back and over the shoulder of the child, as she gently brought first one little arm and then the other down over the chest. The pain was terrible. Mrs

Bennett had to be very careful to draw down the umbilical cord at the same time as she pulled out the baby, in order to prevent suffocation. To help the head pass she held the feet with one hand, and placed the fingers of her other hand in the baby's mouth, gently easing the child out into the world. Mrs Moss stroked Beth's hair and told her it would all soon be over. Both women told Beth it was a blessing that the babies were so small, only just on three pounds each.

Once the second baby and the placenta had been delivered safely the midwife must have heaved a huge sigh of relief, but she also knew that this was a critical period. In anticipation of post-partum haemorrhage she gave Beth a dose of ergot. Ergot makes the uterus contract, often in an extreme and sometimes violent way, expelling the entire contents of the womb. What Mrs Bennett did not know, probably the last thing she would have even considered, was that there was a third child still inside Beth. The ergot had a devastating effect: the pressure the dose exerted on the unborn child most likely caused her tiny heart to stop beating before the almighty contraction, fifteen minutes later, forced her out into the world. The might with which the tiny corpse was expelled caused devastating injury to Beth's perineum, and a massive haemorrhage.

For the next hour Mrs Moss tried to revive the baby, alternately dipping her in and out of hot water and splashing cold water on her little body. She even administered a few drops of brandy in warm water, but it was all to no avail. Mrs Bennett, meanwhile, concentrated all her efforts on Beth. There was a great deal of activity in the little bedroom, with bloodied and soiled sheets and napkins removed for burning in the yard, babies cleaned and wrapped in flannel, and much toing and froing with disinfectants and sterilised wool. Beth lay in the dreamy unconsciousness that follows post-partum haemorrhage, finally free from all pain, suffering and worry, a stream of bright red blood pouring from her. Mrs Bennett saved her life. The pillow was whipped away from underneath Beth's head and placed beneath her legs; a draught of vinegar was forced between her lips, and she came to with dull cramping pains in her womb as Mrs Bennett applied all the pressure she could to Beth's abdomen. Another dose of ergot was administered, Beth was placed on her side and a hot water douche applied.

She would need complete rest, peace and quiet for at least four weeks. In that time she would not be allowed to move at all, especially her arms, and she should not be left alone for the next fortnight at least. First, though, it was necessary for her to be taken to the infirmary for a transfusion. While they waited for the motor cab to come, Mrs Bennett told Bert that his poor wife was not at all well, and that it was very important that her mental strength, as well as her physical strength, had every opportunity to recover. If not she would be very vulnerable to hysterical fits and that could lead to "family unhappiness" and even, at this she dropped her voice, a kind of insanity.

"There has always been a large degree of under
ascertainment of deaths from mental illness...
deaths from suicide...are the leading cause
of maternal deaths overall."

From *Why Mothers Die*, Confidential Enquiry into
Maternal Death Report, published 6th December 2001

While she was still semiconscious Beth was bundled
into a taxi and driven the short distance to the
Victoria Infirmary for a blood transfusion. They told her
there that she would need a major operation, once her
health was restored, which would probably not be for
another three months, in order to repair her "ruptured perineum". It is highly likely that she would have been given
another dose of ergot, and maybe some tincture of opium,
for its painkilling properties and also to help her sleep.
Beth had received what midwives would now describe as a
fourth-degree laceration, extending (between what Beth
would have called her "front and back passages") as far as

the rectal sphincter. She would have been in a great deal of pain and would have suffered much anxiety every time she needed to relieve herself (something she probably experienced, to a lesser extent, for the rest of her life).

By the time Beth gave birth to the triplets in 1919 the practice of giving birthing women an episiotomy was becoming more common (although it was a procedure that doctors, not midwives, carried out). In 1920, the American obstetrician, Joseph de Lee, who regarded childbirth as a "pathologic process" (and was at the forefront of the general transformation of childbirth, over the first quarter of the twentieth century, from something natural into a surgical procedure), published an influential article claiming the benefits of making a cut in the perineal tissue during labour. This was advocated not (as is sometimes believed) in order to lessen the risk of tearing, but to prevent overstraining and overstretching the pelvic floor muscles. De Lee argued that such overextension invariably led to incontinence in most women, as well as a loss of sexual satisfaction (for the woman's partner, that is: many obstetricians would sew up the episiotomy so tightly, the so-called "Husband's knot", that sex became very painful, if not impossible, for the woman herself).

Anxiety about the operation preyed on Beth's already shattered frame of mind. Several times over the next few days she was to confide in Bert her worries about the injuries she had sustained, and fear of the surgery she would have to undergo. He later stated his belief that her physical condition had made a significant contribution to the decline in her state of mind. If so, she was not alone. Vaginal and anal tears are still among the most distressing aspects of childbirth for women, and there has always been a huge fear about them, as well as profound embarrassment. Even nowadays most women prefer not to talk or even to think about the possibility of such damage, making perineal rupture one of the last taboos. In fact the soft parts of a woman are designed to stretch to diaphanous thinness as a baby's head pushes against them, but it is almost impossible for most of us to think of perineal tissue as something alive and elastic.

Procedures for repairing tears have improved immeasurably since Beth's day, yet anxiety about the condition (on the part of both women and clinicians) lingers, and is probably one of the main reasons behind the exponential increase in elective caesarean sections in recent years. If modern women are, understandably, worried about being left incontinent, and about the impact such an injury is bound to have on their libido, their sex appeal, their relationship with their partner, how much more profound (and justified) must these anxieties have been in the past. Eighty years ago such injuries invariably entailed some degree of incontinence and dyspareunia (pain in intercourse) for the rest of a woman's life. Beth would have been aware that the surgical procedure she required might well entail the embarrassment of not being in full control of her bladder, and even her anal sphincter, and an end to any enjoyable sex life for her and Bert. At forty-one, it must have seemed to her as if life was over.

Beth was undoubtedly in a very bad way: severely anaemic and weak from not having eaten properly for the past few weeks, torn to shreds and in agony for much of the time, and extremely stressed and anxious about the future. She was also, of course, suffering the psychological effects of losing not one child, but two, in the space of just eighteen months. In addition to all this she had tiny twins to sustain: babies who might well, in view of their immaturity, have had trouble breathing and digesting, and possibly other physical ailments as well, who would need constant care and were unlikely to ever be asleep for very long or at the same time. Even experienced mothers can find it difficult to establish breast-feeding with twins and especially tiny, premature ones. All day, every day, life revolves around the attempt to nourish them, and is edged with the concern that they are not thriving.

Mrs Bennett admitted that she was as surprised as anyone to find that in spite of all her tribulations Beth, once back from the infirmary, somehow managed to remain cheerful for much of the time. True, she recalled, Beth had a little weep each day, mostly for the little girl she had lost, Maisie, but much of the time she could be found sat up in her bed darning and mending; knitting tiny vests and bootees; stirring pudding and sponge mixture; directing Bert as to the shopping and housework; nursing and making a fuss of the babies; chatting brightly to Mrs Moss, and generally impressing all with her apparently limitless capacity for love and duty and hard work, her ability to cope with all that life had flung at her.

Beth's apparently boundless energy and enthusiasm for life, at such a time, was, of course, far from being the positive sign that those around her took it to be. She was manifesting all the classic symptoms of mania. It would have been hardly surprising if after all she had been through she were not sliding towards serious depressive illness. She may not have been, in the words of one contemporary description of puerperal insanity, "laughing, sobbing, sighing, moaning and talking wildly..." But surely it was not normal for her to be engaged in such a variety of activities so soon after a traumatic birth and serious primary post-partum haemorrhage. Yet nobody in her immediate circle seems to have had any inkling that she may have been in danger. The Broadmoor physician, John Baker, had observed back in 1901 that "... the mental causes [of puerperal insanity] are insidiously at work for many weeks ...", but he also averred that most people were woefully ignorant of the symptoms of imminent mental breakdown following childbirth.

The numerous doses of ergot and pain-killing opiates she had been administered might have played their part in her extreme behaviour. Ergot is derived from a cotton-like fungus which develops in the ovaries of the rye plant. It has a hard, sclerotic, pink body, which resembles a grain of rye, and contains numerous toxic alkaloids. It is from the constituent alkaloids ergotamine and ergonovine that the chemical derivative lysergic acid is derived, and from which, in 1938, Albert Hoffmann first manufactured LSD. Ergot compounds are very close to serotonin and interfere with the serotonin neurotransmitter, reducing the natural levels of the chemical messenger and thus causing the brain to produce extra receptors. The effect of this is to increase sensitivity to existing serotonin in the body, but the ergot compounds also exert a very strong influence on the receptors which in turn can produce the dramatic mood swings, and even hallucinations, commonly associated with hallucinogenic drugs. Could the routine administration of this substance, along with pain-killing opiates (and Mrs Moss's doses of brandy), have exacerbated the ultra-sensitive state of my great-grandmother's endocrinal system? In someone who was already suffering from a great deal of stress, malnourished, depressed, highly anxious, and in shock, is it not likely that liberal doses of a mind-altering substance will be the last straw to break an already fragile central nervous system?

Apart from the whispered conversations with Bert last thing at night concerning her operation, Beth, steadily mutating into the paradigmatic "smiling depressive", neither said nor did anything to arouse the concerns of those around her. In fact, she seemed to be coping so well that they began, fatally, to withdraw the support network. On the morning of Tuesday 26th August, Mrs Bennett, unavoidably detained elsewhere, did not worry too much about not being able to come and spend her usual ninety minutes with Beth. She might have made a different judgement if she had known that the night before Mrs Moss, who had been booked to stay with Beth until the following Saturday, had been called away. Her husband had suddenly and unexpectedly returned from the Front. They had not seen each other for three years, and Mrs Moss was understandably anxious to be with him. As Mrs Moss prepared to leave, at about half-past nine that evening, Beth was sitting up in her bed, laughing and joking about Mrs Moss giving Mr Moss a "proper hero's welcome".

Mrs Moss called in at London Road at some point on the Tuesday morning. She told Beth that she would find another lady to take her place for the rest of the week, and she stayed until nine o'clock that evening. Before she left she made sure that Beth ate a good supper and she bathed the babies in the china washstand basin in the bedroom, so that the mother could supervise and put the little things in their nightgowns. She later recalled that this was the first day Beth had not had a cry in front of her since the birth, which she took to be a good sign. Previously, she observed, Beth had fretted for a bit each day over the little girl that she lost (Maisie, that is, not the stillborn triplet), but not that day. At about eleven o'clock Bert came up to go to bed, and checked that the babies were all right in their cot, positioned next to Beth's side of the bed. Before he went to sleep Beth told him that she was worried that the babies had not had their bath. He, either forgetting or unaware that Mrs Moss had in fact bathed them just a couple of hours before, told her not to worry about it.

At some point after Bert had fallen asleep, Beth left her bed for the first time in ten days. She put on her bed-jacket and her heavy outdoor coat which was hanging on a hook behind the bedroom door (even though it was very warm outside). She either took the babies with her, or she came back and fetched them after she had already been downstairs; all she could remember, she later claimed, was carrying them downstairs, and she was not even sure if she had done that. Certainl, nobody else in the house, not Bert asleep in the bed next to her, not my grandfather or his little brothers in their room across the landing, heard a thing. No footsteps, no babies mewling, no mother urging them to be quiet as she went downstairs and into the scullery.

It was sometime between midnight, when Bert fell asleep, and four-thirty in the morning, when she woke him up in a terrible panic, that Beth must have drowned the twins. The house could still have been in pitch dark or just waking to the first touch of morning light: that was immaterial. She knew every single corner of the little house and could have found her way to the yard in a blindfold. It is even possible that she was sleepwalking. Sleepwalkers frequently use their memory of familiar spaces to move through them without accident. Many an exhausted mother of a newborn baby has had the experience of waking suddenly to find herself standing in another part of the house, with no idea how she came to be there, heating up a feed, or changing a nappy in a half-somnambulant state.

Once in the scullery, Beth must have lifted the latch on the back door before going out into the yard. She allegedly crossed to the shed and removed the galvanised tin bath from its hook behind the shed door. Positioned beside the back door was a rainwater tank about four feet tall with a tap protruding from the top of it; Beth always claimed that she had no memory of carrying, or dragging, the bath across to the tank; she could not explain how she had found the strength to lift it in order that it could sit under the tap; neither did she have any memory of turning on the tap. All she could remember was the feeling of cold water on her hands: it was, she said, the first time she had felt "alive" for ages. She did not remember placing the two tiny babies in the bath, but she did remember hearing the neighbour's donkey shuffling in the shed behind her as she went back through the yard door into the scullery. Then she must have returned to bed.

At about half-past four Bert was woken by a very excited Beth, screaming and pulling at him. "Bert! Bert! Go down and fetch the babies! I've left them downstairs!" Bert was still drowsy as he stumbled out of bed and crossed to the cot. Seeing it was empty, he went downstairs. He moved towards the still open back door, and there, he later testified, he found the bodies of his twin daughters, still in their nightclothes, lying face down at the bottom of the bath. Bert said that he carefully tipped out the water in the yard and carried the bath and its tiny contents inside the house, placing it on the scullery table. He then went back to the bedroom and said to Beth, "You have been and drowned them," to which she replied, "Bring them back. I haven't. I've only been and bathed them…"

Shortly afterwards Bert went and woke up my grandfather.

-13-

"She sat up in bed with a scream of terror. She heard the prison key turn harshly in the door of the cell. She saw the form of the wardress in the doorway....."

From "The Haunted Woman", published in *Weekend Novel* for 1d in 1919

B ert attended the inquest at the Romford Union Offices that afternoon. The district coroner and jury heard his evidence, and that of Mrs Bennett, before adjourning the hearing in order to enable Beth to attend, if she wished, at a later date. Her poor health and extreme mental distress were both noted. The story was picked up by the press: in the next day's *Daily Mirror* it appears, amidst clamourings for the Kaiser to stand trial, and news of the capture of Nurse Edith Cavell's betrayer, under the headline TWO BABIES DROWNED.

It was easy to find the story in the *News of the World* edition of the following Sunday. DEAD TRIPLETS is emblazoned next to the Amusements column, with news of Sir

Johnston Forbes-Robertson's triumphant return to America with his acclaimed lecture on Shakespeare, and the crowds being turned away from a show at the Kilburn Empire.

Curiously, when I first spotted the headline as I spooled through the microfilm, I was overcome with a strong feeling of déjà vu although I am pretty sure I have never seen it before. The black and white line-drawn adverts that surround it were immediately familiar to me: Wrigley's Spearmint Perfect Gum ("look for the spear on every packet"), bargain raincoats for 29/6, Eastern Foam Vanishing Cream ("the cream of fascination"), and, poignantly, a splendid perambulator "the best baby-car ever offered". Bert and Beth took the *News of the World* every week, but their eldest son considered it "dreadful rubbish", only read by "a very low type of person". But I can imagine his anxious teenage self furtively flicking through the pages on that terrible Sunday back in August 1919, dreading what he might come across, the cold shock of realisation that the nightmare was real, the shame of knowing that now everybody knew.

Dr Jeaffreson had ordered that Beth be taken from the house on London Road to the infirmary and placed under "close supervision" (I suppose a euphemism for what we would now call "suicide watch"). She was to stay there for the next seven weeks. When she was first admitted she complained about severe pains in her head and was extremely agitated. Diagnosed by the Infirmary's medical officer as "quite mentally unhinged", she spent the next few days in her own world, keeping up a stream of conversation with little children that only she could see. Puerperal insanity was a well-recognised condition, as we have seen, and the Infirmary staff would have assumed that Beth's illness, irrespective of the legal proceedings against her, would follow the normal course. Drugs were rarely administered: sleep, it was generally averred, was best obtained by a warm bath and a dose of alcohol last thing at night; a generous diet, with liberal amounts of beef-tea, milk, eggs and a few ounces of port wine each day, would soon restore the blood to health and remedy any costiveness of the bowels.

After a period of rest, good diet and fresh air it was expected that most women would return to "full completeness" within three months, although it was usually recommended that they should not resume normal relations with their husbands for at least six months, and that they should have no contact with their babies for the same period. Some women were able to remain in their own homes while they recovered from puerperal insanity, but "constant watchfulness" was advised in order "to protect the infant from [the mother's] insane impulses". If this could not be guaranteed then the mother had to be removed to the infirmary.

The classic symptoms of puerperal insanity were set out in most standard medical text books of the time. E.F. Younger's *Insanity in Everyday Practice*, published in 1917, for example, states that the illness can assume an acute maniacal, melancholic or demented form, and that the maniacal form is the most common. He cites sleeplessness and loss of appetite as early warning signs, both of which Beth suffered from, and complained about, in the final stages of her pregnancy. She did not manifest any of the extreme, lurid behaviour described by Younger ("erotic" actions, "lewd, filthy and blasphemous" talk etc.), but she did complain about headaches, another recognised symptom, and she had also been crying a great deal more than was usual.

If someone around her had been able to recognise the extremely fragile state of her mental health in the weeks leading up to and the days following the birth of the triplets, it is likely that she would simply have been admitted to the Infirmary until she was considered recovered and no longer a threat to her children. All being well, it is likely that, after three months or so, she would have returned to her home, to live out the rest of her life as the loving mother of three boys and twin daughters.

It is extremely unlikely that Mrs Bennett would have had anything other than a lay understanding of mental illness, which in 1919 was not very enlightened, to say the least, or that Beth's GP, Dr Jeaffreson (if he had the opportunity to see her in the period immediately following her confinement) was qualified to diagnose her condition with any accuracy. In 1919 only a very few medical doctors had any clinical understanding of mental illness, and it is doubtful that there were any in attendance at the Romford Infirmary.

At the time British medical schools offered little more than a few hours during one term when student doctors would be taken to visit an asylum, and perhaps given a lecture identifying the advanced cases of "mental disease", categorised as "melancholia", "mania", and "delirium". Apart from the special case of women in the puerperium, and the recently acknowledged phenomenon, "shell-shock", most doctors believed that madness was "caused by" either sexually transmitted diseases (particularly syphilis) or alcoholism. The identification of shellshock, a form of mental disease not ascribable to either syphilis or alcohol, had caused great consternation, and by 1917 it was becoming something of a national scandal that Britain lagged far behind other European countries in the diagnosis and treatment of mental illness. But training of doctors in mental illness remained a low priority for most of the following decade, consisting mostly of visits to asylums to observe "full-blown" cases of insanity. Consequently, there were very few doctors who were able to recognise the early warning signs in people who were about to suffer mental breakdowns.

The coroner resumed his inquest at ten o'clock on the morning of Friday September 19th. Beth was still not considered well enough to attend, although there had been a small improvement in her mental health. The infirmary medical officer reported that she was now able to sit up in bed and to sit in a chair for a short period in the morning. Although depressed, she was sewing, talking quite cheerfully, and had received visits from her husband and the two older boys, which seemed to lift her spirits. She was still, however, very weak physically. The coroner heard evidence from Mrs Moss, who said that Beth had fretted a good deal over the death of Maisie in the days following the birth of the triplets, but had never said or done anything to suggest that she would injure the new babies. Beth was, she said, "very fond" of the baby girls.

When she did finally appear before the coroner, at her own insistence a fortnight later, Beth had to be helped into the hearing by a nurse as she could barely walk. She was still waiting for the operation on her lacerated perineum, and she was not to have the surgery for another five weeks. The coroner took one look at Beth and said that it would not be necessary for her to give evidence. He told Bert to obtain legal aid, saying that it would relieve the jury and himself of "a great anxiety". Bert thanked him and said that he would do so as soon as possible, but he never did. He probably saw it as some sort of a hand-out, and he never liked to take anything. He also hated any sort of paperwork, especially anything to do with income tax, national insurance, anything "official". The Woods always preferred everything to be "cash", and were suspicious of "formality" and "systems". Instead Bert went to his brother and asked him for help in paying for legal representation. To their credit, in spite of all the difficulties in their relationship with Beth, the family rallied around. To his surprise, Bert's mother was extremely sympathetic to Beth. She told Bert that he had to take some responsibility for not seeking help for his wife earlier on.

What sort of pitiful impression must my great-grand-parents have made on the coroner? Beth was desperate to do whatever was expected of her; she made no attempt to dodge justice, or to deny what had happened, although she was adamant that she could not remember very much about the events leading up to the drowning. She struggled into the coroner's court, even though the infirmary advised against it, out of a highly-developed sense of propriety, and an eagerness to co-operate with the authorities. Bert was terrified of the process, but, like Beth, he wanted everyone to think well of them. They both knew how important it was, and now more than ever, to make a good impression. For all their efforts, for all their pride and independence, to the coroner they were objects of pity: a couple of the lower middling sort, obviously out at the elbow, none too well-educated; the little wife a pathetic figure whose health was obviously ruined, and the bewildered husband, eager to make a good impression but completely ignorant of his rights and entitlements. The coroner was also mindful that, according to the expert opinion of the time, the mental aberration that resulted in infanticide (ie "puerperal mania", not just melancholia, which is what we would now term postnatal depression) was often of a fleeting character, perhaps lasting only a few hours. In Beth's case the symptoms would almost certainly have abated by the time she came to trial.

Early twentieth-century medical text books often advised readers to obtain the best legal assistance they could in any criminal cases where mental illness was an issue. Defences had to be properly applied in order for justice to be done. In cases of infanticide, the arguments needed to be applied very carefully: no judge wanted to have to condemn to death a weak, pitiful and frightened woman. So, seek legal aid, the coroner advised Bert, protect your wife and protect the court. This is a very serious situation. It was indeed: in 1919 the only possible charge that could be brought against Beth was murder.

On Friday 17th October Beth, accompanied by a nurse from the infirmary and with a woman patrol either side of her, appeared before the magistrate. She was walking only with great difficulty and appeared to be very thin and extremely weak. On the bench was J.J. Craig, Esq, a local dignitary who owned a large draper's, furniture, clothing and boot warehouse on Market Street. A well-to-do self-made man, Mr Craig was of a type very familiar to Beth; not unlike Mr Gibberd, and the factors Beth's dad had grumbled about when she was growing up. At some point in her life she might reasonably have imagined herself marrying a man like J.J. Craig, but now she found herself before him as he officially charged her with the murder of her two unnamed female infant children. The magistrate heard evidence from Mrs Bennett that Beth was "very fond" of the baby girls, and "a good mother and a very good wife". The arresting officer informed the court that on being cautioned Beth had said "I don't understand" and "I have nothing to say".

She was remanded for a week awaiting her trial. Mr Craig instructed Police Superintendent Howlett to write to the governor of Holloway Prison giving particulars of Beth's condition and the circumstances of her case. He gallantly insisted that she be driven to the prison in a motor cab at the court's expense, and he told her not to worry: she would receive every consideration at Holloway. He asked her if she had anything she wanted to say and Beth told him she was "ever so grateful to everyone for all the thoughtfulness they had shown her".

***

The due processes of law had yet to reach a conclusion, but it was really no more than a formality: the verdict on Beth had already been reached. It was well-known that all women who had recently given birth were susceptible to hysterical fits, especially those whose blood has become poor or whose nerves were already in a weakened state. It was almost inevitable that a woman like Beth would, in such circumstances, suffer nervous collapse and even insanity. One contemporaneous commentator argued that the murder of newborn children by their mothers could in almost every case be "put down to the morbid mental and physical conditions ... resulting from childbirth, especially when taking place under unhappy conditions". The mental asylums of the time were filled with respectable married women from poor or lower-middling backgrounds.

In a 1902 article for the *Journal of Mental Science*, John Baker paints a lurid picture wherein the mother is beset by depression, and "everything looks bleak and dismal, the idea takes hold of her that want and poverty are in store for her and her family. At first an obsession it becomes a delusion: the thought of suicide projects itself into her mind.... She cannot leave the child behind. It must be sacrificed first..."

And that was the official line on Beth, that she killed her twin daughters because she was relatively poor and because she was a woman who had just given birth under particularly trying circumstances. It would also have been accepted in mitigation that the loss of another child a year or so previously and the loss of the third triplet had contributed to the balance of her mind. All of these factors could reasonably have formed the basis of her defence.

Beth's own understanding of what had happened, however, and why, would not have been sought. Nobody asked her why she had killed the babies, what had gone through her mind at the time. Clinicians and legal teams alike would have assumed that she was too confused and inarticulate to be able to offer any meaningful insight into what she had done. Besides, English criminal law seeks solely to establish *mens rea*, that is, the guilty intent of the accused, and whether their mental state is commensurate with the offence with which they have been charged. The principle of criminal culpabiltity is not necessarily interested in the further analysis or exposition of underlying causes.

In 1919 there were about eighteen hundred women prisoners in England and Wales, and the majority of them were incarcerated in HM Prison Holloway, in north London. The grim flinty building, inspired by Warwick Castle, stood on Camden Road from 1852 until 1970, when it was largely replaced with a series of low-rise red-brick units. My grandfather spent a large portion of his adult life living just a few minutes walk away, which always struck me as odd since he had no connection (and neither did my grandmother) to that part of the world other than the fact that his mother had spent two weeks there awaiting trial in 1919. When I was growing up in north London it was often assumed that a girl who wore her skirts too short, ran around with boys, smoked, or chewed gum in public, ran the risk of ending up there. (I lost count of the number of times, during my girlhood, I heard the admonishment: "She'll end up in Holloway if she isn't careful...!")

Oscar Wilde had spent some time in Holloway, but it had been a woman's prison since 1903 and by 1919 was well-established as the place where all remand and convicted female prisoners, as well as those women sentenced to death in the London area, were sent. Many of the suffragettes endured time there, and one of them, Lady Constance Lytton, wrote memorably of the "tier upon tier of cell shutters... a great hive of human creeping things impelled to their joyless labours and unwilling seclusion by some hidden force, the very reversal of nature, and which has in it no element of organic life, cohesion or self-sufficing reason." She was unable, ever after, to pass its high central tower, which could be seen for quite a distance around, "without recalling the sensations which gripped my soul and checked my breath". To her it seemed to be "the quintessence of prison, the very heart of it".

Beth arrived at the prison gates at lunchtime on Friday 17th October 1919. Perhaps she was able to find some solace in Mr Craig's assurances that she would have nothing to fear, as she entered the forbidding gateway and caught her first glimpse of the star-shaped building that lay beyond. On arrival she was taken with the other new prisoners to the reception rooms; any personal belongings she had with her were taken away and their details entered into a book. Then she was given a bath, under medical supervision on account of her injuries, and following that was dressed in the standard uniform: Sister Dora cap, check apron and bib and (as she was a remand prisoner) blue dress with thin white stripes. The prison issue underwear was scratchy and loose-fitting and the stockings black with a tell-tale red strip around the leg. No garters or suspenders were given with them, so they flapped inelegantly around the knees or ankles and had constantly to be pulled up and knotted above the knee. The shoes were black and sturdy but not a great deal of care was taken with the fit of them and quite often they were not even given out in matching pairs. All prisoners were given a yellow badge to wear bearing the number of their cell, and by which they would be referred for the duration of their stay.

Holloway was a hospital first and a prison second and was in this respect quite unique. Because it was so commonly held in the past that women were most likely to commit a crime as a result of some mental disorder, it seemed sensible to put them in an institution where recovery and reform were the guiding principles, rather than punishment. There were two hospitals inside the prison, staffed by thirty nurses, and a medical officer was in overall charge, as opposed to a governor. Dr Sykes took personal charge of Beth, keeping her under observation for the next ten days. In his opinion she was "depressed" and "emotional" but of "sound mind". Her physical health was in "a very delicate state", she was still in dire need of surgery, but here too, she was showing signs of improvement. It was Dr Sykes's opinion that she needed rest and, above all, peace and quiet.

Beth's cell in one of the hospital wings was much like all the others, except for the linoleum floor in place of the flagstones elsewhere in the building. It was about nine feet high and ten feet by six feet wide, with whitewashed walls. The furniture was sparse but sturdy: a hospital-type bedstead, table and chair, mirror and a washstand. There was a little shelf affixed to one of the walls, with a salt pot and tub of toothpowder on it, as well as a copy of the Bible, a pamphlet entitled *Fresh Air and Cleanliness* and a tract called *The Narrow Way*. Also affixed on the wall were two cards: one bore all the rules and regulations of prison life; the other detailed the women's dietary entitlements. In most of the hospital rooms there was a bell, so that nurses could be summoned at any time. The women were encouraged to make their cells as homely as possible, and were permitted to decorate the walls with photographs and picture postcards if they wanted to.

Constance Lytton (in Holloway about ten years before Beth) may have found prison life a terrible shock, but then she was used to a far higher level of comfort than many of the women who found their way inside the walls of Holloway. Even outside the hospital wings, the prison had the ambience of a hospital, and the prison wardresses looked more like nurses than guards. Lytton found them to be "fine-looking women" with "beautifully-kept hair" who "held themselves very upright". However, conditions in the seven different halls varied greatly. E Hall, where remand prisoners were housed, had horrified at least one of the suffragettes placed there a few years before, because it was filthy and invested with mice. It was, however, preferable to F Hall, where prostitutes infected with VD were placed: it was unthinkable that any decent, respectable woman would be housed there.

Beth was preoccupied with worries about how the children and Bert were faring, and what the outcome of her trial would be, and she was expressing a great deal of remorse and grief. As far as Dr Sykes was concerned, these feelings were not of a heightened type, indicating that the acute phase of Beth's insanity was passing, and she was no longer in any danger of committing suicide. The expression of guilt and remorse, as long as it was not too morbid and obsessive, would also have been taken by him as a positive sign. She kept herself to herself, staying in her cell as much as possible, spending most of her time sewing, weeping, and, on occasion, talking with the wardresses. She found them to be very kind women who did their best to reassure and comfort her.

The bell went at ten-past six every morning and breakfast, consisting of bread and marge, porridge and a cup of tea, followed at five- and twenty-past seven. Most of the prisoners had jobs to perform, but Beth was relieved of work duties on account of her delicate health. Dinner followed at twelve o'clock noon and was quite varied. Each day prisoners were offered one of the following: beans and bacon; preserved, roast or boiled beef; boiled beef and dumplings; stewed steak; haricot mutton; hot-pot; Irish stew; bacon or meat pie; meat pudding; boiled or roast mutton; sea pie; shepherd's pie; brown soup. There was always treacle pudding for afters. At ten to six a supper of bread, margarine and tea was served. Between eight and nine pm, those women who had work duties had an hour's rest before the lights went out.

***

The coroner's verdict was that each of Beth's babies had died as a result of "suffocation from drowning", after being placed in a bath of cold water, by "its"[sic] mother. Once he had the official notification, Bert was able to go and formally register the deaths of the twins and then he could collect the little bodies from the mortuary for burial. He did all of this on the Monday following Beth's admission to Holloway, 20th October 1919. The funeral was held two days later.

Once again my grandfather found himself trooping past the workhouse and through the pretty gates of the cemetery. The family stood around the grave where Maisie had been laid to rest nineteen months earlier, and watched as the two little coffins were placed along side hers. This time there was no Burial Society money. No reputable company would insure a child before it was three months old, mindful of the temptation that would be placed in the way of that increasing legion of desperate people who would do anything for a few bob. Bert carried the tiny coffins to the grave edge, one under each arm; his brother saw to the rest.

It was a shock for me to discover that the grave of my grandfather's little sisters, the locus of so much sorrow and loss, is just an empty space: a neat strip of mown grass in Romford's Crow Lane Cemetery, between two well-proportioned headstones belonging to strangers. I suppose that Bert, who worked very little that year, was unable to find the money for the stone; I am sure that his family would have offered to help with this, as they were to do with so much else, but maybe, even with Beth out of the way, he declined out of some sense of loyalty to her. Perhaps it had really rankled with her that the Woods had provided the plot for Maisie, and the whole business had proved too much for Bert, always caught in the middle. Perhaps it was simply that Bert and Beth could never bring themselves to see to a stone for Maisie. After all, the time since her passing had been fraught with so many other concerns: Beth's mental health had declined so dramatically, and then within a year she had been expecting again. Perhaps, when the twins died, nobody could bear to bring it all to mind again, and the time slipped by, and it was eventually, tacitly, agreed that the whole thing was best forgotten. That would be in keeping with the *modus operandi* of my grandfather's family, indeed of most people of their time. Certainly it would have been a course that matched the advice of most medical professionals. The standard clinical recommendation in those days was that "putting it all in the past" and "trying to forget" was the best remedy.

The grave spot has not, however, been neglected: there are plenty of tatterdemalion, crooked graves in Crow Lane (as there are in all cemeteries), where the grass and weeds have claimed back what is theirs, overthrowing patterned stonework and elaborate statuary. But the grave wherein Beth's daughters are lying is an oasis of tidiness, manicured and tended, despite the fact that, as far as I know, nobody in the family has visited it for decades. Was it, in fact, ever visited, in the way that graves belonging to less traumatised families than my grandfather's are visited by the bereaved? Were there ever Sunday afternoon rituals, standing around the little mound of lawn, clutching untidy bunches of the garden flowers Beth loved so much, foxgloves, daffs, sweet williams...? Nobody alive now seems to have any memory of ever being taken there, although, when prompted, my mother remembers that as an old lady, years into the future, Beth had liked to walk around cemeteries. She used to say that she found them peaceful. Did she ever wander about Crow Lane looking for the unmarked grave? Did she even know where it was? It is highly likely that the family, on the advice of doctors, thought it best never to let her know, in order to safeguard her from developing a morbid fixation, and succumbing once again to the mental illness which always threatened to reclaim her.

No names for the twins appear on either their birth or death certificates; on the official court documentation they are each referred to as "a certain female child lately before then born of her [Beth's] body and not then named". But they *were* named, just as they were loved and cuddled, kept clean, fed, clucked over and worried about. Their names and ages are entered on the cemetery list. The Crow Lane register gives the number of the plot, the date of burial and, in strict alphabetical order, the name and age of the deceased. The entry for Kathleen May (Maisie's full name) was easy to find and just before her on the list, against the same plot number, was the first of her sisters; a few names further down the list I found the other one. The two name-less little ghosts who have hovered over my mother's family for so long were Queena Maud (in honour of Bert's youngest sister) and Freda Kathleen. When Beth nursed her baby daughters, and kissed their downy heads, she was not only thinking of her own darling little Maisie; she was also remembering Mrs Gibberd's little girl Freda, all those years ago back in Crystal Palace.

-14-
Up from the earth these mosses creep,
And this poor thorn they clasp it round
So close, you'd say that they were bent
With plain and manifest intent,
To drag it to the ground;
And all had joined in one endeavour
To bury this poor thorn forever.

From *The Thorn*, by William Wordsworth

Beth was finally arraigned at half-past ten in the morning at the Essex Autumn Assizes held in the Shire Hall, Chelmsford, on Friday October 31st 1919, before Justice Bray. It was six weeks since she had drowned her babies. She was still very weak and needed a great deal of assistance from the two wardresses who accompanied her before she was able to climb into the dock. A chair was provided and she was allowed to remain seated while the charges were read out. She must have been terrified. There was still an outside chance that the jury would find her guilty and she, and the family, would have to endure the horror of hearing the death sentence pronounced against her. The legal people in the courtroom would have known that were that to happen, there was every chance that it would be commuted by the Home Secretary, but nobody, certainly not Bert and Beth, could have known for sure.

Beth only spoke to confirm her identity and to plead "not guilty" to the indictments of wilful murder of her two "unnamed infant daughters". The counsel for the prosecution opened the proceedings by running through the litany of sad events which had been Beth's recent life. He was remarkably sympathetic in tone, and much of his statement could easily have come from the defence counsel. He detailed the difficult birth, the dead baby, the still mourned-for four-year-old child, the operation which Beth still desperately needed, her confused mental state, the distress...

He told the all-male jury that the real question they would have to make up their minds about was the state of mind of the defendant at the time the deed was committed. He assured them that when they considered the circumstances, and what Mrs Bennett and Dr Jeaffreson would tell them of her words and demeanour after the tragedy, they would come to the conclusion (subject to the judge's directive) that when Beth had committed the act she had not been of sound mind. The prosecution team had clearly taken the view that their task was to keep Beth from the condemned cell. They wanted to make the proceedings as straightforward as possible for all concerned, thereby sparing the jury and the judge any distressing decisions, and the court as a whole any unnecessary scenes.

The evidence of Dr Jeaffreson confirmed that the babies had died within ninety seconds of being placed in the water. He had very little to say about the state of Beth's mind before the drowning, as he had not been called to her until after. When he saw her on that occasion she was extremely agitated and confused, and "did not seem to have a full knowledge of affairs as they then were". Then Mrs Bennett, the midwife, took the stand. In her testimony she offered one or two small but telling observations.

First, she noticed that Beth's overcoat had been removed from its normal place on the back of the bedroom door, and was draped over the end of the bed when she was summoned to the house by my grandfather. She also noticed that the kettle on the kitchen range had not been boiled that morning. Mrs Bennett did not say as much, but it is clear that to her mind Beth had not been intending to bathe the babies at all. Why else would she have put on her overcoat, unless she was aware that, to some degree at least, she was going to go out into the yard? The babies had been bathed the previous night by Mrs Moss, not in the tin bath which hung in the shed, but, being so tiny, in a vitreous washbasin which lived in Bert and Beth's bedroom. Even supposing Beth really had been intending to bathe the children, and in a confused state of mind had thought of the tin bath, why had she not thought to boil up the kettle first? What sort of mother washes tiny newborns in cold rainwater?

None of Mrs Bennett's hints needed further elucidation by either the prosecution or the defence: there was no doubt that Beth had drowned the babies, and all that needed to be decided was her state of mind at the time she drowned them. The counsel for the defence concluded his opening argument by declaring that this was "probably one of the saddest cases it was possible to conceive".

Beth was, he said, an excellent mother and an excellent wife. The loss of her little girl eighteen months before "had caused her great distress" and affected her "right up to the time of these events". He submitted that "while in a very weak state of health" she made an attempt to do for the babies "what she deemed to be necessary", and that she had not the "faintest intention to injure them in any way whatever". The deplorable result of what she did was entirely a "misadventure".

Then Bert was called as a witness, and asked to go through the events of that morning one more time. He said that Beth hardly seemed to know what she was doing and when he told her of his discovery she did not appear to realise that the babies had been drowned. "My wife worried about the operation," he told the defence counsel, as if by way of explanation. "She is a good and affectionate wife and mother, Sir," he told the judge. "Her sons and I should like to have her home again." But that could not happen. Next, Dr Fraser from Holloway Prison stated that what had occurred was the result of "a temporary aberration" and that, in his opinion, Beth was now depressed but of sound mind. That was undoubtedly the case, but even so there were now very few options open to the court, and allowing Beth to go home was certainly not one of them.

His Lordship then turned to the jury, directing them that "murder" meant "the intention to kill", and if they found that the accused did acts which, presuming she was sane, would "show that she intended to kill the children", then it would be their "duty to find her guilty of murder", before they came to the question of whether she was "responsible" or not. He made it clear that he could not see that there was any question of misadventure. Although he did not state as much, it is clear from his inference that as far as he was concerned there was no evidence that Beth had taken the babies down into the yard in order to bathe them, still in their nightclothes, in cold rainwater: like Mrs Bennett he was of the opinion that she had taken them into the yard in order to drown them. If, however, the jury thought that the deaths were the result of a calamitous accident then, he counselled, they should find her "not guilty". If they found her guilty as charged, then they would have to say whether they believed that at the time "she was responsible for her act".

After just a few minutes deliberation the jury found Beth guilty of murder and that at the time of the act she was not responsible in law for her action. Mr Justice Bray ordered that she be kept in custody during His Majesty's Pleasure.

***

When, in 1883, a respectable middle-class woman, Elizabeth Agar, had set fire to her baby (an action which had led to the poor infant's death), the medical supervisor of Broadmoor had stated in court that the lady was medically sane. She should, he argued, be spared not only the death sentence, but the stigma and distress that would result from being received into his care. The judge agreed with him and wrote to the Home Secretary, pointing out that the poor creature would "go mad altogether" if she were to find herself committed to the insane asylum. However, no such objections were made in regard to Beth: like most women of the lower middling sort, who had been found guilty of killing their children in the nineteenth and early twentieth centuries, she was committed to Broadmoor, and destined to stay there until the authorities could be persuaded that she was no longer a threat to society. In practice this could have meant that she would remain there for decades. A good many of those women sent to Broadmoor around the same time as Beth was, could be found, years later, whiling away their days in the mental health institutions to whence they were generally transferred in the 1960s and 1970s.

When I first started researching this story, I felt sure that

Beth's incarceration in Broadmoor must have been the product of family legend. It seemed almost ludicrous that this would be her fate, and much more likely that she had been sent to Essex gaol, or the local asylum at Brentwood. Broadmoor, to those of us who know it chiefly as society's last resort – the final destination of serial killers, the Ian Bradys and Peter Sutcliffes of the world – seemed so extreme. Working on the basis that what I had been told must have been wrong, it consequently took me a long time to discover precisely what had happened to Beth after the judge had pronounced sentence on her. The newspapers all ended their coverage at that point, and none of them made any mention of Broadmoor, or any other prison or hospital. I realise now that this was because, back in 1919, there was no need to spell it out to their readers. Anyone reading about the case would have known exactly what Beth's fate was likely to be.

Broadmoor was opened in 1863 to house ninety-five female criminal lunatics, and it soon became the most likely destination for women found guilty of murder, whether they were found to be insane, temporarily insane or otherwise deemed not responsible for their actions. By the end of the nineteenth century the total female intake was approximately two hundred, of whom around one hundred and twenty had been convicted of the murder of their own child or children, most of them in those critical first weeks following childbirth when allegedly in the grip of temporary psychosis, diagnosed as puerperal insanity. It is highly likely that many of these women were technically sane at the time of their committal. In 1893 the then Home Secretary declared of the hospital, "there are a number of patients who are not really insane, and are treated... with all consideration and kindness..." On 4th November 1919, my great-grandmother, Beth, became one of them.

When the writer of *Sidelight on Convict Life*, George Griffith, visited the hospital (like Holloway, Broadmoor was not considered to be a prison) in 1901, he regarded it as "at once the most interesting and the most depressing" place he had ever been. It would not have changed very much by the time Beth arrived there eighteen years later. He depicted a "mental and moral wilderness" that was entirely at odds with the beauty and tranquillity of its surroundings, picturesque farmland edged by a "dark belt of fir forest. One of the most charming spots that I have ever seen in England or out of it..."

Then, as now, Broadmoor sits on top of a hill, overlooking the small town of Crowthorne in Berkshire, with a high security wall separating it from the rest of the world. Behind the wall, Griffith was surprised to find immaculate terraced lawns, where inmates strolled past "dreaming" and "carrying on conversations with imaginary hearers". There were also tree-lined avenues down which they were free to wander, laughing to themselves, sheltering beneath fruit-trees from sun, rain and whatever else they feared, and there were neatly laid out, colourful flower-beds, tended by the "blood-stained hands" of the patients. The hospital had no towers with armed guards atop them, no chief warders with swords, or officers with batons, no handcuffs or chains, and no flag-paved exercise yards. The surroundings may well have reminded Beth of childhood visits to the local mansion, Wakefield Lodge, in Potterspury, with her Sunday school. All there was to remind the visitor that this was not some country park estate, was "the unlocking and relocking of solid doors and iron gates". There was also, the rest of the time, an unnerving silence which the wary visitor expected to break at any moment.

The inmates tended to keep themselves to themselves, little mingling and conversing, hardly appearing to take much notice of one another at all. After all, you had no way of knowing who you might chance upon; striking up a casual conversation with the pleasant-looking woman sitting next to you might prove hazardous. Griffith made the mistake of doing just that and discovered to his horror that the well-dressed lady doing a gentle bit of tatting, who "could have graced any drawing-room in the land" with her calm eyes, well-coiffured hair and "delicately-bred" features, had in fact cut her children's throats. Another good-looking, buxom woman, in very good spirits, told him that she had been sent to Broadmoor fifteen years before, after she had set fire to the bed in which her babies were sleeping.

Broadmoor's inmates were patients of the State, not its prisoners. Their uniform was like that worn by workhouse inmates, which is to say plain and simple, but without the tell-tale broad arrows of the penal institutions. They did not live in cells, but rooms, arranged in long corridors. The rooms were small, but comfortable and clean, affording pleasant views of the grounds. At the end of each corridor, however, was a great portcullis which grated open and clanged shut at frequent intervals.

As in wider society, there was a hierarchy: two, actually. Firstly, as mental illness is no respecter of social status, there were a certain number of inmates who were of the "best class", in possession of incomes which ran into four figures. Their trustees were permitted to provide them with little "extras", and they did not have to wear the uniform. Secondly, there was a system of stratification ordained along the lines of mental health. The "convalescents" were the respectable, one might say "genteel", mad, those who were tranquil in their behaviour and appearance and who were probably not really "insane" at all. Then there were the "actively insane", quiet and orderly most of the time, but liable to "outbreak" at any moment and so kept under constant surveillance. At the bottom of the pile were the "stark raving mad", who were kept out of sight in the dread "Black Blocks". Here the furniture was bolted down, the plates and cups were made of tin, not china, and the cutlery purposely blunted. These unfortunate women spent their days huddled in corners or dragging themselves up and down the corridors, scraping their bodies against the walls. Their hair was untidy, their eyes wild and staring and they whimpered horribly. In Broadmoor Beth, for the first time in her life, found herself at the top end of the social system: she was a convalescent and a very good, considerate and hard-working one at that.

Was she just going through the motions? Did she have to make a conscious effort, I wonder, to surrender to the system of the place? Or did it suit her, this strange locus of oblivion and displacement, where those whom the rest of society wanted to forget could spend the remainder of their days in obscurity, unchallenged, unrecalled, shut away and altogether lost in the hopeless task of trying not to remember who and why and what had brought them there. In the female wing women sat about the corridors heads bowed over their knitting and sewing. In the common rooms they read or played the piano, "thinking the thoughts", avers Griffith, "and dreaming the dreams of a world that is not ours..." A world of never-ending shame, regrets and grief: a world with no peace, no respite and no future. It was also, to some extent, a world with no past: clinicians were not interested in hearing from the women in their care why they might have killed their babies, and they unquestioningly accepted the women's own claims that they had no clear memory of the events leading up to the killing, the killing itself, nor its immediate aftermath.

Dr Sullivan, Broadmoor's medical superintendent at the time Beth was admitted there, was in no doubt that in the majority of infanticides, the mother suffers "a more or less complete blankness of memory for the crime..."

This is sometimes followed by a period during which "relevant delusional ideas" develop, wherein the mother attempts to justify her actions by claiming she believed, for example, that the baby was "dying of some awful disease, or would grow up deformed..." Some mothers clung to their belief that their children had died of natural causes, and one wonders if, at a time when doctors were entirely ignorant of the existence of SIDS, some of them at least were telling the truth.

Sullivan was of the opinion that the amnesia, at least, was genuine, "and the most probable explanation of it would seem to be that it results from the unconscious repression of the painful memory of the crime." In this, Sullivan demonstrated that he had some familiarity with what were in 1919 ultra-modern ideas about mental illness. But for the most part, although there had been some experiments with hypnosis in the treatment of shellshocked soldiers, psychotherapeutic understandings of mental illness in Britain were considered unorthodox. And most clinicians, Sullivan included, would still have held that insanity had a physiological basis: the curious behaviour observed in the mad was the manifestation of changes taking place in the brain; and treatment, therefore, focused upon the relief of symptoms rather than in attaining a deeper understanding of the patient's psyche. In general terms, when a patient stopped acting and looking as if they were mad they may be considered "cured".

Indeed the various types of mental illness were always

described in terms of *physical* manifestation: thus a depressed patient was slow in her actions, and a manic one in a state of constant activity. Doctors concentrated their efforts on observing a patient with a view to determining whether or not she was now restored to normality, and able to return to her duties as a wife and mother.

Although patients did talk about their lives, and clinicians sometimes recorded what they said, the practice was far from the "talking cure" associated with Freudian analysis. While the patient talked, the doctors were observing her behaviour and speech patterns, looking for tell-tale outward signs, rather than hoping to uncover latent causes. In some cases talking about the past could be taken as a bad sign by clinicians. A patient who insisted on going over the events leading to her committal, for example, might run the risk of being judged as excessively morbid and obsessive, and therefore still in the grips of insanity.

It is important to remember that by the time many of these women, including Beth, reached Broadmoor they were no longer certifiably insane, and therefore were of limited interest to doctors trained in the observation of extreme cases of dementia, by which reputations and careers were enhanced. These women were extremely melancholic, and full of regrets – they would have talked about "feeling queer" and "bad with their nerves"; of everything being "black" and "full of trouble" – but to the clinicians this sort of ill-educated discourse merely confirmed the original diagnosis and showed that they were now over the worst.

On occasion Beth expressed her terrible guilt at what she "must have done" (there was no recollection of having done it, but she accepted that she must have "because everyone said she had done so"). She sometimes wished that she had been given a death sentence rather than "King's Pleasure": she repeatedly stated that it was only the thought of her "dear little boys" that kept her from being "so reckless" with her own life. Her remonstrations were very typical of those heard every day by the doctors; they regarded them as evidence that a woman was no longer insane, but precariously balanced on the knife edge of normal feelings and depression. She needed to be observed, because at any moment she might fall into the abyss of emotional dementia, inhabited by a large section of the population of every chronic asylum. She might spend years sitting in a corner, expressionless, motionless, making no attempt to occupy herself and apparently noticing nothing. All hope gone, all life extinguished, forgotten.

The so-called "liquid coshes" of our own time, were not in use in Broadmoor in the early part of the twentieth century. It was not until the 1940s and 1950s, the boom period for pharmacology, when mental hospitals began to acquire their distinctive smell of paraldehyde, that tranquillisers and thymoleptics became the preferred treatment. Early forms of mood-modifiers and neuroleptics had been in limited use since the 1890s, and there were occasions when cannabinoids and opiates might be administered to calm and control the overexcited, but these were the exception rather than the rule. Their routine use was not considered to be especially effective, and in the case of depressives, it had been observed that such drugs could actually worsen their symptoms. It was not until the 1940s, following the discovery that oral doses of lithium carbonate, a mineral salt, could improve their condition that severely depressed people received any hope of a cure. The doctor who attended Virginia Woolf during her 1915 breakdown, Sir George Savage, had earlier expressed an unwillingness to administer sedatives, having observed that narcotics "not only do not cure, but... in many cases, act injuriously, making possibly curable cases incurable." His opinion was very influential and most of the standard textbooks of the time support his claim.

As for more drastic forms of treatment, such as surgery, although the discovery had been made in the 1880s that docility could be induced in some patients by severing the frontal lobes, brain operations did not become prevalent in the treatment of the mentally ill until the 1930s, and electroconvulsive treatment was not administered until 1937. In the period immediately following World War One, for all but the most maniacal and dangerous patients the regime in Broadmoor was relatively benign: cold baths and wet-packs were among the more extreme treatments reserved for those requiring restraint. Beth was probably given laxatives, as costiveness of the bowels was considered very detrimental to mental wellbeing, and she might have received medication to regulate her periods, if that was necessary; other women might have been given medication to suppress lactation, but for the most part their treatment focused upon increasing their physical strength, through diet and rest. If, however, women were admitted during the transient stage of their delirium, then judicious administration of a narcotic, such as hyoscyamine was recommended. This is a derivative of henbane, one of the deadly nightshade plant family; a cannabinoid, it inhibits the neuro-transmitter acetylcholine, thus sedating the central nervous system. Beth would almost certainly have been given this during her initial stay in the Romford infirmary, but it is unlikely that it would have been thought necessary by the time she came to Broadmoor. By then her "transient delirium" had long since past, and she was in the grip of a much more enduring depression, vividly described by Savage as "a saturated solution of grief". She believed herself to be irrevocably ruined, and a cause of profound misery to all those around her. It was a conviction from which she would never entirely free herself.

***

Although the birth-rate in England and Wales had been declining since the turn of the twentieth century, during the years of the Great War the numbers of illegitimate babies shot up. Throughout the period 1914-1920, there was a corresponding rise in the numbers of babies drowned in rivers, and discarded in mine shafts, hedges, ditches, pigsties and church porches. By 1918, the mortality returns for illegitimate children stood at more than twice that of legitimate babies.

In October 1919, as Beth prepared to stand trial, the Birmingham board of governors drew attention to the urgent situation regarding "unwanted babies". With the average cost of a foster-mother running at eight to ten shillings per week, there were few options available to those women who found themselves in a desperate plight.

Legitimate babies were also in increased danger, as mothers – some widowed, others the wives of destitute returning soldiers – came to the conclusion that they had little choice but to spare their children uncertainty and hunger.

Some babies died not at their mother's hands, but, ironically, as a result of their mother's efforts to sustain them. During the war there was a marked reversal of the trend for women to stay at home. This situation was stimulated by the increased demand for women in the workplace when so many men were away at the Front; it was sustained during the Depression which followed, when more and more women were forced to find any sort of work at all in order to keep themselves and their families from starvation.

Many had no choice but to leave their babies in woefully inadequate and largely ill-regulated environments and the notorious baby-farms which had shocked a previous generation began to make an unwelcome return. The case of Nurse Grace Thompson during 1918 reawakened some awful memories. A child left under her care at the Blackheath baby centre, while its mother worked, died suddenly and was found to have a suspicious mark on its forehead. Nurse Thompson claimed the infant had fallen in its cot, but then it was revealed that six other babies had incurred similar injuries and three of them had also subsequently died. It emerged that Thompson was a violent drug addict, and she was found guilty, though insane. She was one of Beth's fellow inmates at Broadmoor.

Closer to Beth's Romford home, the case of the "Leytonstone Baby Farmers" (a couple called the Hatchards) horrified readers of the local and national press during the long, hot summer of 1919. Several of the babies left in the Hatchards' care died in circumstances of unbelievable neglect. The couple's twelve-year-old daughter testified that her mother would instruct her to play the parlour piano loudly in order to drown out the cries of the filthy and starving babies locked away in an upstairs room. The couple were convicted of manslaughter a few days after Beth drowned her twin daughters.

Such cases upset the general public far more than the "sad" and "pitiful" stories, such as my great-grandmother's. When Elsie Kathleen Smith, accused in 1919 of the attempted murder of her newborn child, was sentenced to four months in Holloway, the Women's Freedom League collected thousands of signatures on a petition and organised a march to the prison on her behalf. The protestors were outraged that a woman such as Smith, clearly vulnerable and unhinged, but not a serious threat to society at large, could receive such a harsh punishment. Similarly, in the wake of the Leytonstone Baby Farm scandal, two of Beth's neighbours wrote letters to the newspapers expressing their outrage and indignation that a "respectable" and "fond" wife and mother could be dealt the same measure of justice as the "purposefully evil".

There was still great sympathy elicited for those whose lives had been blighted by puerperal insanity, or sheer economic desperation, but in the years dominated by the Great War, any waste of human life had assumed a special resonance. The declining birth rate and the untimely deaths of healthy babies, whether through poverty, neglect or murderous intent, became a serious issue, and the value attached to promoting healthy human lives consequently increased.

In 1915 Hugh T. Ashby, a distinguished paediatrician, addressed the topic of infant mortality on the grounds that the subject was "of paramount importance at the present time." "The State," thundered Ashby, "needs all the healthiest and strongest children it can obtain in order to keep abreast of the struggle for existence among the nations and races which is now going on and is likely to go on and even to become more strenuous in the future..."

Concern for the future survival of the race was of central importance to most social health reformers in the years following World War One, spurring the development of the powerful eugenics movement during the same period. Needless to say, it was only the mentally and physically healthy whose lives needed to be safeguarded: it followed that the "unfit" and "feeble-minded" should be prevented from breeding at all costs. The 1914 Mental Deficiency Act made provision for the establishment of separate colonies for the mentally and educationally "sub-normal". When Marie Stopes opened her first birth-control clinic in Upper Holloway, north London, in 1921, she was largely prompted by her concern that the "low-grade stocks" were breeding in an "ever-increasing ratio in comparison to the high-grade stocks, to the continuous detriment of the race..."

***

Sometime after her committal, Beth's sons were taken to a photographic studio and posed in their best clothes for a portrait for her to keep in the hospital. The baby, Alfie, stood grinning on a chair, too little, at three, to grasp the significance of the occasion, but old enough to be missing his mummy; the middle boy, Stan, twelve years old, smiled sadly in front of a potted palm; my grandfather, a man now, seventeen, stood straight and tall in his tweed suit and affected an air of genial indifference as he looked out over the heads of his little brothers.

Their home life had been radically altered: they were used to a high order of daily care in a spotless home, and

281

unstinting attention and delicious food from a mother who adored them. In Beth's absence, Bert's mother (as Beth might have said with a bitter edge to her voice) came into her own. She was by now affecting all manner of quite grand mannerisms, such as driving down to the post office in her little pony and trap and waiting outside as the clerk came onto the street to hand over her old age pension in person. Still, she and her unmarried daughter took Beth's sons in and saw to it that they were fed and watered. Bert, you see, had quite gone to pieces. He hardly worked and spent most of his days in a terrible state, not troubling to shave and wearing his trousers over his un-collared shirt, or, worse still, his combinations. Beth had been the centre of his life, and with her gone there seemed little point in him carrying on. He lived only for the possibility that one day she would be sent home to him once more. He felt it was her rightful place to be with him and the boys.

Over the next year my grandfather, now that the horses were no longer a going concern, helped to keep the family going, and it seems as if he really did begin to mature. Freed from the necessity of working with his dad, he began to exploit his contacts on the millinery stalls in Romford market. Soon he was earning as much as 18/- a week, more than his dad had earned as a father of three just before the war, and within another year he had achieved his goal of a motor of his own. He divided his spare time between playing Mozart in the silver band and losing himself in the dark of the Lawrie cinema, "the place where everybody goes". There he thrilled to weekly episodes of *The Claw*, "A Novel of South African Life", *Adventures Among the Cannibals,* and *Bolshevism*, "A Stirring Super-Film Drama of Intense Interest". No doubt he also succumbed to the delightful enticements of Mabel Normand "in a Romance of a Bathing Suit: *Venus Model*".

And so it was that the first year without Beth slipped by. In December 1919 the Romford and District Chamber of Commerce initiated the town's first shopping carnival, with all the shop windows of the town "attractively dressed", many of them containing free gifts. The very wet weather did not affect the excitement surrounding the week's "malletting", which it was hoped would show that Romford was every bit as good as London. At the final planning meeting the town's MP, Sir Alfred Yeo, complimented the Chamber of Commerce on its progress and enterprise and wished the shopping carnival the greatest success. The proceedings ended with the singing of "God Save the King". The opening ceremony took place in the Victory Palace, South Street, attended by a large number of townspeople, including many of the principal residents. A week later the council bought Cottons estate from the landlord for £25 an acre: it would not be long before the great house was finally demolished: there were few living in Romford now who could have afforded such a fine abode. In the week of Christmas it was calculated that the sum of winter Out Relief to the poor was between £235 to £290 per week and steadily creeping up on the previous year.

The New Year began with a whist drive for the unemployed and a "pretty performance" of *The Water Babies* to raise funds for the Sunshine Home for Blind Babies. There was concern about the numbers of wives abandoned by their husbands and left to the charge of the Romford Union.

By the spring rent-round Bert had rallied enough to move himself and the boys to a new home, 81 Market Place, right in the heart of the town. This was a little cottage with one big room downstairs, a little scullery out the back and three small bedrooms upstairs. It was the very last building on the north side of the market, part of the block containing the market offices, and situated right next to the loam-pond and the old village stocks. Directly in front, a few feet away from the front window, was the place where the cattle were weighed before auction. Bert had come to the conclusion that it was necessary, for the sake of all of them, to leave London Road with its terrible memories far behind, and he certainly did not want his poor dear Beth to ever return there again. Bert saw to it that every little thing of Maisie's which had survived the fumigation was moved with care. My mother remembers that there was still a room set aside for her things in the little cottage in the 1950s, even though the little girl herself never lived there, and had by then been dead for more than thirty years.

It is about this time, once he and the boys were settled in Market Place, that Bert began to write his letters asking for Beth to be released. He wrote first to J.J. Craig, the magistrate who had sentenced Beth, then he began writing to Sir Alfred Yeo, the MP, and then, finally, he wrote to the authorities at Broadmoor.

Bert was not an articulate man, and it is not impossible that these were the only letters he ever wrote. The letters that remain on file are simple, and very respectful, in style: they ask that Beth be allowed to come home ("her sons are missing her ever so much, especially the youngster, and so am I"), and emphasise her good qualities ("she has always been a most affectionate and good wife and mother"; "I have never known her to harm any living thing"). Others wrote letters too. Beth's older sister Martha wrote (in her best former assistant-school-teacher's hand) to the medical supervisor at Broadmoor: she told him she thought it "quite unfair" that her "poor sister" be incarcerated, since "there was never any trouble in the family before this" and she was sure that Beth had been simply "overcome" following the loss of her little girl the previous year. Bert's brother also wrote, on business letter-heading bearing his telephone number (he was one of the first people in Romford to have a telephone), giving assurances that he would do all he could to ensure that his brother would be kept "steady", and able to provide a good home for Beth and their sons, should his sister-in-law be permitted to return home.

However, the decision to release patients from the hospital was entirely the responsibility of the secretaries and under-secretaries of state for England. And, like most of the families of women admitted to Broadmoor, Beth's appears to have been ignorant of the formal procedures for applying for a patient's discharge. No formal application to the Home Office was made by her family on Beth's behalf until 1921, by which time she had been in Broadmoor for nearly eighteen months.

Once a family had been apprised of the bureaucratic process, infanticide cases had the best chance, out of all Broadmoor admissions, of being granted a conditional discharge. Jonathan Andrews has found that sixty-eight per cent of the women in his sample were conditionally discharged, as opposed to forty-five per cent of men in the same period.

A woman's age and physical condition were important factors in considering discharge applications: a woman nearing menopause, who was unlikely to become pregnant ever again, stood a far better chance of being released, sooner rather than later, than did one who still had several years of childbearing potential.

The Broadmoor supervisor, Richard Brayn, wrote in 1901 of the "undesirability" of allowing infanticides to have any more children, but he recognised that they presented a perplexing ethical problem. Public opinion would not tolerate the idea of having these women sterilised, and it was hardly just to keep a healthy woman in an asylum until she was past child-bearing age. Nonetheless, women patients were generally not considered as suitable for discharge unless it was certain that menstruation and other gynaecological issues had been regulated.

On occasion the local police force might visit the family home in order to assess its suitability as the future refuge of a discharged mental patient. The social and moral respectability of the family, its economic circumstances, the level of educational attainment of the woman and her husband were all factors to be considered. Judgment could be harsh: if the authorities were minded to look down upon a woman and her home life, for whatever reason, they could condemn her to spend decades in hospital, irrespective of whether she constituted a danger to anyone else or not. Of prime importance in this respect was any indication of hereditary insanity in the individual's family.

In his 1902 paper for the *Journal of Mental Science*, "Female Criminal Lunatics: A Sketch", Dr John Baker, a physician superintendent at Broadmoor, states that hereditary insanity was one of the six main factors which "may mitigate against the chance of a recovery" in respect of infanticide cases admitted to Broadmoor. He further estimated that hereditary insanity had been a significant feature of one quarter of Broadmoor's infanticide admissions. The testimony of relations, friends and even neighbours of the patient might be sought, and letters written to and by the patient were often intercepted by the hospital authorities and scrutinised for evidence of a family history of madness.

Luckily for Beth, there was no formal evidence of any insanity or criminal tendencies in her family, and nobody willing to come forward to argue otherwise. I have looked for the evidence as assiduously as the Broadmoor authorities must once have done, and can confirm my great-great aunt Martha's avowal that "there never was any trouble in the family" before Beth's own tribulations.

***

On April 17th 1921, during Beth's final year in Broadmoor, a twenty-one-year-old unmarried factory hand from Leicester, Edith May Roberts, suffocated her newborn daughter by tying a camisole around the baby's mouth. Then she hid the body in a large box under the flock mattress on her bed in her parents' home. When discovered, she confessed immediately, telling her father: "I was frightened and ashamed". Roberts later changed her story, claiming the baby had never breathed and had felt cold when she kissed it moments after the birth. The family doctor tried to help her out with the old tried and tested submission that it was perfectly possible the girl was "unconscious from the pain she suffered", and consequently, "might not realise what she was doing." The defence counsel suggested that "whatever she did was done in the frenzy of agony and pain through which she was passing and therefore she was hardly conscious of her own acts at the time and consequently not responsible".

The jury found her guilty of murder, but recommended mercy. On hearing the guilty verdict, Roberts nearly fainted and said in a feeble voice: "I am very sorry. I didn't intend doing it..." But the judge placed the black cap on his head in any case and proceeded to intone the death sentence. The terrified girl collapsed and her dreadful cries and moans filled the shocked court room. She had to be carried from the dock, and several spectators also fainted.

There was an immediate furore. "A Mother" wrote to the *Leicester Daily Mercury* the next day summing up the nation's mood. "Why was not the man there [in the dock]?" she demanded, going on to suggest that "this girl should be treated with kindness and sympathy – in a home if you like – where she can be nursed back to health... Let me say that she is not as wicked as married women who deliberately prevent motherhood..."

A petition of ten thousand signatures was collected and sent to the Home Secretary demanding that the death sentence against the "girl mother of Hinckley" be commuted, and a week later Edith Roberts was reprieved. The editor of the *Leicester Daily Mercury* thought that she should be entirely let off, as she had surely suffered enough, and he joined the clamouring for a change in the law. Within a year the Infanticide Act, 1922, was on the statute book. From then on it would be impossible for a woman to be condemned to death for the killing of her baby, if it was found that "at the time of the act or omission the balance of her mind was disturbed by reason of her not having fully recovered from the effect of giving birth to the child or by reason of the effect of lactation consequent upon the birth of the child..." The lesser charge of manslaughter would apply in such cases, and a two-year prison sentence (rather than a spell in a mental asylum) would become the standard punishment.

A few months before the formal change in the law, on the 4th December 1921, Beth was allowed to come home, conditionally discharged into the care of her husband. There is nothing in the accompanying paperwork to say that she was cured, but then there never was anything to cure her of. Not as far as the doctors in Broadmoor were concerned anyway.

Family legend has it that it was Bert's brother who, by using his money, and status in Romford's business community, somehow secured Beth's release from Broadmoor, but it was not. It was Bert who promised to look after her, if he and his sons could only have her home again. They loved her so very much; they missed her something rotten; was it possible that she might be allowed to come home now? She was surely as sorry as anyone for what had happened and Bert would see to it that she was taken care of and no harm would be done. He had kept the little home on Market Place as clean and tidy as he could, and when the constable came to call he saw that the three boys were turned out very neat, in their best clothes, shoes polished to a high sheen, faces and hands scrubbed pink, hair slicked back into gleaming helmets. He tried his best, did Bert, to make a good impression. And it worked.

The Romford that Beth returned to was fast becoming

part of the modern world, but enough would have remained that was familiar to her: the excitement occasioned by an ox or carthorse rampaging through the market; or a cow breaking into somebody's garden; in the workhouse men were still breaking stones; on the London road barefoot children still called out to the passing charabancs "Throw out yer mouldies!" There were more of the drifters finding their way into the courthouse or the workhouse, having had their bellyful of life on the streets, of going in the mud for halfpence at Hungerford, of stealing fruit at Covent Garden; those who were born in the back of a travelling hawker's van, or who came home one day to find the room empty and their parents gone, who earned a few bob by holding horses on the street, or by picking rosehips.

By the time she was released, Beth, though still only forty-three, had transformed into the "nice old lady" who, a year later, introduced my grandmother to my grandfather, following a chance encounter at a county fair. She began to wear her greying hair in a thick flapper bob, and to dye it red in an effort to keep up with the fashion, but she was spindly and rickety beyond her years. She became one of those old girls who complained about her aches and pains: the sciatica which was like hot knives in her poor old legs, the stiffness in her old bones; and the weather (always either too hot or too cold or too wet). She no longer stopped to talk to people when she went to do her shopping, for, as she often said, she had nothing to say to any of them. In truth, of course, she had plenty to say but nothing that anyone else could be expected to understand. Besides, she was used by now to people ignoring or avoiding whole topics of conversation to spare themselves, and her, embarrassment. She liked to look out of the window onto the market square and watch the world pass by. She spent her days in baking, making, mending, cleaning, keeping her cottage neat, and filling it with knick-knacks and bits of lace. In June 1922, she won first prize for her fancy crochet work, second prize for her fruit cake and third prize for her loaf at the Mawneys Bank Holiday Fair. In September work was begun on the arterial road.

She still worried. She worried all the way down through the years about everything and everyone. When the next war came she worried about Bert's youngest brother losing his job and all the others like him who "don't know what they will do". She worried about her daughter-in-law and grandchildren evacuated to their family in Pontypridd. She was glad to hear from my grandfather that his own business was bearing up, but even so she was worried that the war meant ruin for a good many other people. She worried about her thirty-seven-year-old son going out in the blackout. She never stopped worrying. That's what mothers do.

Beth never beat the depression she had probably suffered from for most of her life, in one form or another. She died of a pulmonary embolism on the 15th September 1957, just before her seventy-ninth birthday. She was on the public ward of Warley Hospital, Brentwood, known until four years previously as Brentwood Mental Hospital. By then dear old Bert had been dead for eight years. In the interim Beth had remarried, to the widower of her older sister Martha, a man both sisters had known since they were girls back in Potterspury. (Beth and her sisters had remained close throughout everything.) With her sisters gone, and Bert too, Beth simply thought it would be sensible to move in with Martha's widower. They knew each other, liked each other, had a common past back in Stony Stratford, and they were both very lonely. Besides, it would make living a bit cheaper. But there was no way that Beth could entertain the idea of living in sin. Most people in the family took this as yet more proof of Beth's "eccentricity" or "barminess", depending on who you talked to. My mother was a teenager when the wedding took place in June 1953 – just after the Coronation – and her Grandma Wood asked her to stay overnight at the little cottage in Market Place. All night mum could hear the newly-weds giggling through the thin wall that divided the rooms.

Beth's "awkwardness", however, soon proved too much for her new husband to cope with. He was no Bert. She began to make wild accusations that he was seeing another woman at the Darby and Joan Club (which nobody could bring themselves to believe, since he was nearly eighty). Her mind did what it always threatened to do – it began to unravel. Once my mum went to visit, bringing a bunch of flowers for her grandma. She was astonished when Beth put them straight in the rubbish bin, murmuring to herself, "Oh, they're dead, dear. Quite dead."

Another time, she tried to set fire to her petticoats. A family council was held, my grandfather's brothers and the new husband thought it would be in Beth's best interest to have her committed, and my grandfather went along with them. The decision broke his heart. He remembered the promise his dad had made to always look after his Beth, and he felt that he had let them both down.

In the hospital she stopped dying her hair until it was snowy white. Sometimes she had no idea who her beloved son and granddaughter were when they came to visit. After she passed on a year later, her widower moved in with his "fancy woman". My grandfather never forgave himself for doubting his mum. In the crossfire of accusation, guilt and blame that ensued, he severed all connections with his two younger brothers and never spoke to them again. They were all dead, within five years of one another, by the early 1980s. My grandfather willed himself to die, following his admission to hospital for a routine operation. It was the first time he had ever had any illness in his seventy-six years, and he simply let it defeat him. Like his shoemaker grandfather he suffered a massive stroke, then another and finally a third, which took him. His last words to me were to tell me to take care of myself, when he noticed that I had burnt my finger on the stove.

***

What can I salvage from this lost life of my great-grand-mother?

A memory of cold water splashing on hands, reviving, in a dingy backyard one dawn, long ago, when the sun was already hot, and the thick air smothering all other feeling, all senses. A donkey shuffling in the shed behind: the only witness. A loving husband, who sometimes let you down, true enough, but who, when it mattered, knew just what to do. Stunned, heartbroken, but he was thinking of you when he fished the babies out of the tank and placed them in the tinbath, and told everybody not to judge: that you had only been doing what you thought was necessary. What you thought was right.

My grandfather was a curmudgeon, who ruled over all of us with his threat of withdrawing that which we most wanted from him: his love. But he was in the end a great lover: of women, of literature, of wandering, of doing a job properly, of nice clothes, of rich gravy and thick dripping, of my mum and her brother, of my siblings and our cousins, of me. Whenever I was with him I felt loved and safe and special. Somebody must have taught him how to do that.

When I had my babies I was at various times nuts: over-emotional, anxious, terrified, lonely, inept, but I also knew moments of quietude and contentment, of mutual absolute love, of adoration, passion, even, for these boys of mine. And on those occasions when I was able to short-cir-cuit the lunacy pumping through my endocrinal system, ricocheting off my neurotransmitters, inhibiting the flow of serotonin, I knew that all I had to do was love them and that part of it was never, ever difficult. After all, as I now know (after my own perilous negotiation of the Scylla and Charybdis of motherhood: passion and boredom; resentment and acceptance; hope, joy, fear, worry, despair and of course, finally, love itself), I am lucky to come from a long line of loving mothers who did whatever they had to do to keep that love alive, so that it could be passed down to all the mothers who would succeed them. All I had to do was follow their example.

And it therefore follows that the family memory I most cherish, although it is not mine, is of a little skinny mother being lifted high in the air by her big strong man-child, and spun around and around against the sky. And she is laughing and laughing and laughing.

ACKNOWLEDGEMENTS

A huge number of people contribute to the research and writing of a book like this – one which touches on so many different areas of expertise.

Thanks to the following individuals for generous contributions of time and knowledge: Suzanne Bardwell, Home Office; Brian Evans, Romford Local History Group; Chris Pickup, Department of Health; Andrew Roberts, Lecturer in Sociology at Middlesex University, for his interest and help with bibliography; Dr Tony Ward, Principal Lecturer in Law, De Montfort University, for generously sharing his considerable knowledge; Peter Webb, Potterspury's local historian; delegates and speakers at the symposium, The Unforgivable Crime, held at St Antony's College, Oxford in September 2003.

Thanks to staff at the following institutions: the British Library; British Library Newspaper Collection (in particular the porters at Colindale for their unfailing good nature in heaving all those huge bound volumes onto the lectern for me); Buckinghamshire Studies Centre; Essex Records Office; Family Records Centre, London; London Metropolitan Archives; National Archives; Northampton Records Office; Staffordshire and Stoke on Trent Archive Service; West London Mental Health Authority.

And warmest thanks to: Phil Steer for creating a vivid impression of a long-lost Romford; Annie Williamson-Noble for her assistance with research, and companionship on trips to Northamptonshire and Buckinghamshire; Trudy White, Emma Boniwell; Rosie and John Burgess and Sharyn Pountney for being great sounding boards; Aurea Carpenter and Rebecca Nicolson, at Short Books, for their support, guidance and trust; my husband, Robert, for understanding and encouragement; and my father, Tom Busby, who died during the latter stages of the book's gestation, but has left his mark here as everywhere else in my life.

Finally, I could not have written this book at all without the inestimable contributions of my uncle, Mr PW Wood, and my mother Wendy. Their precious memories, unstintingly shared, form the essence of this work, and, in so far as writing it may be considered an achievement at all, the credit is at least as much theirs as it is mine.

Needless to say, all mistakes, errors and omissions are my own, the result of my wild enthusiasms and erratic tendencies, memory lapses and poor handwriting. I apologise sincerely for any inaccuracies, errors and omissions – they are all unintentional.

A NOTE ON SOURCES

My chief sources have been primary: public records, contemporary newspapers, and family correspondence, photographs and memories.

I also read a great many books written between 1870 and 1920 on obstetrics, insanity and criminality, as well as numerous marital guides, works on motherhood and various medical compendia of the time. Most of the secondary sources I have used are acknowledged in the relevant sections of the main text, but there are a few general works which I would like to single out for special mention.

Advice to Women, by Florence Stacpoole (1911) was particularly useful in offering an almost uniquely feminine viewpoint of early 20th-century obstetrics. Maud Pember Reeves's *Round About a Pound a Week* (1913) and M.L Davies's *Maternity: Letters from Working Women* (1915) offered great insights into the world of my great-grandmother.

Of the more recent works consulted: Peter Webb's *Potterspury* (Potterspury Village Appraisal Group, 2001) and Brian Evans's books on Romford (*Bygone Romford*, Phillimore & Co Ltd, 1988, and *Romford*, Sutton Publishing, 1998) have been invaluable sources. Tony Ward's article "The Sad Subject of Infanticide: Law Medicine and Child Murder" (*Social and Legal Studies*, 1999) was very helpful in placing infanticide in a legal and socio-historical context. As were the articles by Tony Ward, Hilary Marland and Jonathan Andrews in Mark Jackson's excellent volume *Infanticide:*

Historical Perspectives on Child Murder and Concealment, 1550-2000, (Ashgate, Hants, 2002). Lionel Rose's, *Massacre of the Innocents* (Routledge & Kegan Paul, 1986) is still a good starting point for those interested in the subject of infanticide and a good source of figures and further reading.

Information on the other topics covered in this book has come from a great many sources, but the following works were of particular use:

Crystal Palace: *The Rise and Fall of the Biggest Ever Glass Container,* C.A. Bell-Knight (1977); *The Crystal Palace Park of 1854: a Guided Tour,* Christine H. Northeast (1979).
Domestic Service: *Every Other Sunday,* Jean Rennie (1955); *Below Stairs,* Margaret Powell (1968); *Yes Mum – No Mum: Life in Domestic Service,* Maeve and Ben Chapman (1991)
Horse-dealing: *Confessions of a Horse Coper, containing many curious revelations in horse dealing,* Balinasloe [pseudonym of Frederick Taylor], (1861); *West with the Tinkers,* Cledwyn Hughes (1954)
Lace-making: *Lace Villages,* Liz Bartlett (1991); *Bobbin Lace-making,* Pamela Norman (1983).
Shoe-making: *The Art of Boot- and Shoe-making,* J.B. Leno (1885); *The Boy's Book of Trades* (1865)

I'm A Teacher
Get Me Out of Here!
Francis Gilbert
1-904095-68-2

At last, here it is. The book that tells you the unvarnished truth about teaching. By turns hilarious, sobering, and down-right horrifying, *I'm a Teacher, Get me Out of Here* contains the sort of information that you won't find in any school prospectus, government advert, or Hollywood film.

In this astonishing memoir, Francis Gilbert candidly describes the remarkable way in which he was trained to be a teacher, his terrifying first lesson and his even more frightening experiences in his first job at Truss comprehensive, one of the worst schools in the country.

Follow Gilbert on his rollercoaster journey through the world that is the English education system; encounter thuggish and charming children, terrible and brilliant teachers; learn about the sinister effects of school inspectors and the teacher's disease of 'controloholism'. Spy on what really goes on behind the closed doors of inner-city schools.

My Brief Career
The trials of a young lawyer
Harry Mount
1-904095-69-0

My Brief Career, Harry Mount's hilarious account of his hellish year as a "pupil" – a trainee barrister in The Temple – has all the horror of a Dickensian tragedy and all the charm of Bridget Jones' Diaries. An exposé of what goes on behind the ancient walls of London's inns of court, this fascinating story dares to reveal the grim secrets of one of England's most archaic institutions. This is a book for everyone who has ever thought they might want to become a lawyer.

In case of difficulty in purchasing any Short Books
title through normal channels, please contact
BOOKPOST Tel: 01624 836000
Fax: 01624 837033
email: bookshop@enterprise.net
www.bookpost.co.uk
Please quote ref. 'Short Books'